Answers to Your Everyday Money Questions

Answers to Your Everyday Money Questions

LORRAINE L. BLAIR

HENRY REGNERY COMPANY
Chicago, Illinois

Manufactured in the United States of America
Library of Congress Catalog Card No. 68–31463

CONTENTS

FOREWORD: What Good Money Management Can Do for You 1

1. Handling Money Is Everybody's Job 17
2. What Does Your Financial X Ray Reveal? 33
3. Are You Really a Smart Shopper? 51
4. Using Credit Successfully 63
5. Your Family and Money 81
6. What Everyone Should Know About Insurance 97
7. Saving for Short-Term Needs 113
8. Saving for Long-Term Goals 129
9. What It Really Costs to Own a House 141
10. Wise Investing Needs Time and Training 157
11. Yes, You Can Become a Millionaire! 173

INDEX 191

Answers to Your Everyday Money Questions

FOREWORD What Good Money Management Can Do for You

There is probably not a day in your life when you do not think about money or what it can do for you. As you perform your daily routines, you need money to buy the goods and services necessary for your very existence. Whether you work for an employer or are in business for yourself, you work for money —and how much you earn is often used as a measurement of your success in your career. You need money for food, clothing, shelter, and other comforts and necessities and conveniences for yourself and your family. When you plan what to do with your life, money will probably play a vital part: pay for the vacation you have been longing for, provide the medical care needed by someone you love, pay for your own home, give you security in your old age.

Because money is the medium of exchange in our culture, almost everything in our lives hinges upon its effective use. Obviously, if you earn much of it, you can enjoy more good things than if you earn very little. If you spend it wisely, you can obtain more of what you want than if you have no ability to use it satisfactorily. If you invest it prudently, you will be putting it to work productively, again enabling you to enjoy more of what you want.

Consequently, money is perhaps the most important tool we have to help us to achieve personal satisfactions and to attain our goals. It is a tool we can use to enrich our own lives and to better humanity. Statistics prove that people without money worries are healthier and live longer than those with money problems. They have fewer mental, emotional, and physical problems. Money, therefore, when it is used rightly, is not something to be despised.

I have never been able to understand why our schools and colleges traditionally ignore the fact that money, when properly used, can help humans to realize their lifetime ambitions and achieve important satisfactions. Courses in the management of money would teach people how to free themselves from immediate hand-to-mouth concerns so that they could concentrate on the cultural pursuits in life. We should not overlook the fact that our cultural heritage—the great works of music, the artistic and architectural masterpieces, even much of the great enduring literature—was made possible largely because wealthy persons were willing to sponsor artists, writers, painters, and other craftsmen. Before such sponsors could serve as instruments of culture, however, they had to have wealth. We respect their memories because they used their money to enrich human lives.

Many people avoid discussing the subject of money because they think it is evil or vulgar to try to make more effective use of money. Some quote the Bible, saying that St. Paul said, "Money is the root of all evil," but Paul said no such thing. He said, "The *love of money* is the root of all evil" (I Timothy 6:10). And there is a great deal of difference between *loving* money for its own sake and *using* it to accomplish good for oneself, one's loved ones, and mankind in general.

My purpose in writing this book is to try to move you as far from loving money for its own sake as you can go. In the finance courses I have taught for more than thirty years, I have tried to stress one point to all my students: there is great good to be accomplished by learning to *use* money in the most effective way. I often point out that a young man attending a school for carpenters is not taught to love a hammer and saw, but if he does not learn to appreciate what those tools will do for him, how their proper use can enable him to earn a living, he will not be adequately equipped for the career he seeks.

Let me emphasize my philosophy regarding money: it is a tool to be used to reach your personal goals. If my students learn how they can use these tools to achieve the best results, they have learned one of the most important things that contribute to their sense of accomplishment, self-confidence, and personal happiness and add to their overall enjoyment of living.

How you use this tool is entirely up to you—a matter for personal choice alone. If you know the facts and circumstances surrounding money and its use, you will be able to make choices about every use to which money can be put—to spend or save, to spend on this or invest in that—with intelligence and understanding.

As proof that a person with know-how about money matters is properly equipped to make choices suiting his or her own desires and ambitions, let me cite the cases of some persons who, I feel, have used their understanding for their personal satisfaction and accomplishment.

One woman I know lives in modest circumstances. While she earns a good salary as an office manager of a secretarial service, she watches her pennies. She does so in order to buy all her clothing from some of the more expensive shops in Chicago. "I know I pay a great deal more for my shoes, hats, and dresses than I could buy them for elsewhere," she says, "but the service I get at these shops and the feeling of security I get knowing that I am always wearing the right things are worth more to me than any satisfaction I could get by buying my clothes for less."

A young secretary in the same office brings her lunch to work every day but spends $10.00 every three weeks on a haircut instead of the customary $3.00. "Robert does my hair just the way I want it, and I think the difference in price is worth it," she says.

A third woman is a college professor who has lucrative consulting assignments as well. She chooses to live in an extremely low-priced apartment and makes all her purchases at discount houses and bargain-basement stores. "As soon as I have saved enough money," she says, "I want to take a few years off to travel and write."

I mention these as examples of the different ways in which people use their money. These three women have one thing in common: they are doing what they want, and they know what they are doing. They realize that they are making a choice and that almost always some disadvantage, inconvenience, or discomfort is a part of the choice they make. The woman who buys at only the most exclusive shops knows full well that she pays a great deal extra for the privilege. The young secretary knows that she must work almost one complete day just to pay for her haircut. The college teacher chooses to do without comforts she could easily afford to obtain the satisfaction that achieving her ambition will give her. Each one knows exactly what is happening, and each one is making her own choice. I say, "More power to them all."

In this book my aim is to show you what happens when you earn, save, spend, or invest your money in certain ways—to give you the underlying facts you must have in order to make your own decisions. For example, I can tell you that when you buy an automobile, you might be able to save $100 or so simply by paying for it by means of a loan from your local bank instead of through the credit plan the car salesman puts in front of you. If you choose, you can decide to take the salesman's plan because you like his blue eyes or the charm of his smile. I would tell you to go right ahead, but just realize that you are paying $100 for the privilege of enjoying his charm.

Another example: if you want to take an outside job to augment your family's income, I do not say you should or should not. But I can show you the economics at work—the fact that you may not earn as much as you think you will, on account of the increased deductions from your pay, that you may even lose money on the deal if you have children whose care has to be paid for.

To sum up: I want you to know the pros and cons of what you are doing when you spend or save or invest your money, and I want this knowledge to help you accomplish the goals and objectives you have set up for yourself.

Over the years I have had the opportunity to consider the "financial X rays" of hundreds of individuals and couples having trouble making ends meet. Almost without exception, whenever a person tells me he is spending more than his income, he wistfully expresses the notion that all his problems would be solved if only he had more income—an additional thousand dollars a year, perhaps, or even only a few hundred dollars more. If there is one thing all poor money managers have in common, it is the idea that they do not earn enough. Rarely does it occur to them that the real cause of their trouble is that they spend too much on things that do not fit in with their major objectives.

I have often heard the refrain, "Our troubles would be over if we had a larger income," from couples in the $8,000-a-year bracket. But even more frequently I have heard it from those with annual incomes of $12,000, $20,000, even $30,000 and more. Persons with low incomes may have some basis for their statements. However, I have found that, in general, even when these persons look to an increase in income as the way to solve their financial difficulties, the relief they get is only temporary. Sooner or later the real cause of their problem—bad spending habits, failure to plan and set goals, and lack of self-discipline—catches up with them, and then they are just as badly off as before. Of course, you need more than a goal. You must know how much this goal will cost you and how you can go about getting the money you need to achieve it.

To convince you of the truth of what I say, imagine that you can sit by my side and listen to the stories of those one would think would have not a financial worry in the world—

those with incomes of $20,000 a year or more. One of the saddest tales of financial woe I ever heard came from a woman whose husband had a take-home pay of $31,000 a year, or roughly $600 a week. Many people in lower income brackets might think they would have trouble even *spending* $31,000 over one year's time. Nevertheless, this woman said that she and her husband not only had no trouble disposing of the $31,000 take-home pay, they were also running up debts at the rate of about $4,000 a year.

I asked her to tell me precisely what their income was going for. I suggested that we might uncover some expenses that could be cut drastically, if not eliminated entirely.

"I wish I could believe that, Mrs. Blair," she replied. "My husband and I have been over this ground again and again. I don't see how we can cut our expenses by more than a few hundred dollars."

I persuaded her to list her expenses anyway. She recited item after item that was "absolutely necessary," that could not be cut out without ruining their standard of living.

For example, inasmuch as her husband was a vice-president of a large nationwide corporation headquartered in Chicago, they "had" to maintain an apartment costing $600 a month on Lake Shore Drive. Couldn't they find a less expensive place? No, they "needed" this one in order to maintain the husband's standing in the community. Any place less elegant would give their friends and business associates the impression that he was not successful.

They also "needed" a country place, since it was not fashionable to spend July and August in the city. So they rented a house with a lake view at a cost of $2,500 per year.

They believed that unless they sent their ten-year-old to a private elementary school, he would not be able to get into a good preparatory school and, later, a prestige university. Hence, it was "necessary" to spend $2,000 a year on tuition.

Since this woman and her husband thought they had a position to maintain, they felt it would be a great social sin if either appeared in public in anything but the latest fashion: another $2,000 a year "had" to be spent to keep their wardrobes up to date. Nor could they be seen driving a low-priced automobile. Therefore, their automobile expense (for depreciation on a luxury car, insurance, cost of operation) was almost twice what it would have been if it were not "impossible" for them to own a compact car.

On and on went the woman's recital. On evenings out, they "had" to dine at expensive restaurants and sit in the most expensive theater seats. When they took trips, they "had" to travel first class and stay at the most expensive hotels. Her husband "had" to eat lunch at the best places, "had" to have one or two expensive drinks before his meal, and "had" to leave a more generous tip than average, all in order to display his affluence.

As this woman continued, I could see that she really believed everything she said. It would do no good, I realized, to tell her that she could bring their spending in line with their income very easily, by doing without a summer place, buying a smaller car, and cutting down on expensive entertaining. What first had to be changed was this woman's attitude about what constituted necessity in her life. I pointed out that most people would consider the height of luxury items she regarded as absolute musts. But my comments had no effect. She insisted that she alone could tell what she "had" to spend money on.

I told her that if she ever wanted to be a good money manager, she had to learn to put first things first, to decide what was most necessary, what they really wanted most, not only in the present, but also in the future. I hoped that my advice would take hold, but it was obvious that her desire to impress everyone with the fact that they were successful and could afford all the good things in life was a stronger motivating force than anything else.

My observations were confirmed later. Her husband received a substantial promotion and his take-home income shot up more than $10,000 a year. If I had not known the couple's background, I might have surmised that now they would get out of debt and begin to save money. However, before long I learned that they had moved to an even more expensive apartment, were renting a larger country house, owned an even more prestigious car, and were making periodic trips to Europe (all first class, of course) and buying clothes from the most expensive European designers. I do not know this couple's current financial status, but it seems probable that they are just as much in debt, just as worried, as when their income was only 75 per cent of what it is today—or, for that matter, as when the husband earned only a small fraction of his current income.

On the other hand, I know couples whose joint income has never exceeded $8,000 a year, but who can retire at sixty-five and lead comfortable lives, secure in the knowledge that they will not face want for the rest of their lives. I know of one woman who arrived in America forty years ago at the age of eighteen with only $21.00 to her name. She met a butcher's apprentice, and they were married. He became a full butcher a few years later, but all his life he worked for a salary that never averaged more than $110 a week. The woman remained at home until their four children were raised. The family always had a clean home in a respectable neighborhood, always had enough food and clothes, and met whatever expenses it encountered in the course of living. Yet hardly a week passed that the husband and wife didn't put something away into savings, even if only a few dollars. Every so often, they bought shares in a mutual fund. At sixty-five, the husband retired with a guaranteed income as great as he had ever earned in his lifetime. Their children are all well educated and own their own homes.

As this couple's story suggests, the amount of your income is considerably less important than the way you handle it. This is true on every economic level. I might make one exception—in cases, for instance, when a couple earns barely enough to provide food, clothing, and shelter in the most basic form. However, even some families forced to live on relief as a result of hardship or ill fortune have managed to do so in some comfort without going into debt. I recall the case, not long ago, of a man who had been on welfare for years but who had saved enough to build up an equity of $80,000 in common stocks. He had many different ways of saving money. For instance, he never bought newspapers or magazines; he spent part of his day at the nearby public library, reading the newspapers and magazines available there.

I am not suggesting that you live at the level of people on welfare. I do suggest, however, that most Americans have incomes sufficiently large to enable them to obtain the necessities of life, and some reasonable comforts, conveniences, and luxuries, without going into debt for them. If your family income is more than, say, $9,000 a year, I think that you can manage on it. You might not be able to save much, but you can at least avoid debt.

As the experience of the couple with the $31,000 annual income suggests, one of the most important things you must do is to recognize realistically what is necessary for you in life and what is merely a convenience or a luxury. If you want to indulge in luxuries, you should recognize that you are making a deliberate choice—deliberately choosing this luxury because it provides you with a greater degree of pleasure than the satisfaction you would get from knowing that you are living within your means and avoiding going into debt. When you make a deliberate choice, with a full awareness of the consequences and a willingness to accept them, you are acting as a mature, intelligent adult. If you choose to buy caviar today, you know you are living high. You do not then wring your hands and cry that your income is not sufficient for "necessities."

Over the course of the years, I have met people with a wide variety of ideas about how money can be spent most wisely—people ranging from an old-style New England woman who never spent a cent unless it was necessary and who considered even common conveniences such as television to be sinful luxuries, to a couple who went to the racetrack every payday knowing that the results of their night's activities determined whether they would live on beans or steak in the week to come.

Strange to say, these people were good money managers, in the sense that they were using money for their own purposes and were not being used by it. I do not agree with either of these philosophies, as should be clear, but I do not question the right of the individual to hold them.

The trouble with most people who have money difficulties is that they want two things. They want to cater to their desire to have more and more of the good things in life, and at the same time they want to avoid money problems. They do not realize that they can't have both. So many financial demands are made upon us that not one of us—not even a Rockefeller—can afford to buy all that he might like. We must draw the line someplace. I read recently that a well-known millionaire has been flying to and from Europe in the economy-coach section. Apparently, even he has had to decide at some point what to spend his money on and to avoid spending it on everything possible.

The key point in your education in handling money effectively should be your awareness that you are constantly required to make choices—to choose this item or that one, or none at all. If you choose the expensive dress, you will have less money for shoes. You must decide for yourself what you want most, and you must face the reality that no choice will be completely satisfactory. Some element of sacrifice will be involved. Buy the expensive dress, and experience the distress of dipping into savings to pay for it, going into debt, or doing without something else, such as lunches for a few weeks. Avoid the expensive dress, and you may also experience a feeling of sadness because you will not enjoy the satisfaction you would have had wearing it. Neither choice will be 100 per cent satisfactory. The question then becomes one of deciding which is more important to you. Once you learn to analyze the pros and cons of any decision and to make a conscious and deliberate choice between them, you will be able to live more contentedly with your decision, whatever it may be.

Like most people, I once thought that persons with high incomes are better money managers than those with low incomes. Experience has taught me, however, that this is not necessarily so.

I have been impressed time and again with this simple fact: those who manage their financial affairs well do so because they make it their business to do so. They have a clear understanding of what the proper use of their financial resources will do for them, and they have a strong determination to pursue that goal. To state it another way: good money managers give a high priority to financial solvency and a good outlook for the future, and they have sold themselves on the benefits they will get from such solvency. I have often told my classes that anybody, whether a dropout from elementary school or a person with degrees from the world's greatest universities, can manage money well if he really wants to.

The word that sums up what I am saying is *motivation.* It docs no good to daydream about how nice it would be to have a large bank account, blocks of common stock or real estate, or any other attributes of great wealth. Financial security is achieved not by idle dreams but by a clear desire for it, by the willingness to learn how to get it, and by the stern willpower to achieve it.

Many times someone comes to me and says: "First, I'd like the latest model car and enough clothes for all the seasons and all occasions, so that I'd never feel that I wasn't dressed properly for business or any social event I attend. Of course, I'd like a good home, well-furnished with modern (or antique, or colonial) furniture, the sort of place my friends would envy. I'd like to travel—possibly to someplace like Europe in the summer, Florida or Mexico in the winter. And I'd like to give my children a good education, a wedding and reception that would be the high spot of their lives, plus a little nest egg to help them get started in life without having to make so many sacrifices."

At about this point, I interrupt and ask: "Never mind about the distant future. Are you saving money today, doing anything to help you achieve your distant goals?"

"Well, I'm not doing so well right now. Money just seems to pour through my fingers. I go into a store to buy one thing and leave with other items I never intended to buy."

My next question is: "Do you have a plan to help you get all the wonderful things you'd like in the future?"

More often than not, I get an answer like this: "To tell the truth, I made up a plan a few years ago, found it too hard to live by, put it in a bureau drawer, and forgot about it."

This conversation, which has been repeated in roughly the same form dozens if not hundreds of times, illustrates a fundamental difference between those who fail at money management and those who succeed. The failures would like to succeed at spending and saving their incomes, but something always gets in their way. They were ready to start saving, but then they saw some summer clothes priced so low they could not resist buying them. They set some cash aside, then they were slapped with an insurance bill they had forgotten about. They worked so hard all year that they decided they deserved a good vacation, so they spent all their savings. Relatives were coming from out of state for a week's stay, and their living room furniture suddenly looked shabby and in need of replacement. It was so easy to get credit on new furniture, and the salesman was so courteous and patient, that they spent half again as much as they had expected to spend and put themselves into debt for two years. And so on and on.

Persons who have such experiences almost always take the position that something forced them to buy what they did not want. In their view, the cause of the problem was not themselves. They act as though the insurance company should send them regular reminders that a bill will be presented six months from now, that relatives should visit only when a house and its furnishings are in excellent condition, that a salesman should not try to persuade them to buy more than they can comfortably afford.

They will deny this, but it is true that the reason they fail financially is that they really do not want to be financially secure. They would like to be free of money problems, of course, but they do not want it enough to make sacrifices, endure hardships, forego pleasures of the moment in order to achieve their long-term goals.

As part of their lack of determination, people who do not handle money well generally have two defects: first, they are not realistic about what they need to live well; second, they are afraid of "what people will think."

If we took two persons with identical incomes, one with financial security he has built by himself and the other unhappily running into debt, I could virtually guarantee one difference between them: the one in debt has many things he considers to be absolute necessities that the second easily does without because he puts first things first.

For example, one woman convinces herself that in order to retain her job, she *must* dress in the latest fashion and never be seen in clothes from a few seasons back. She *must* live at a fashionable address, although she might obtain equally comfortable quarters elsewhere, at substantially less cost. She *must* shop at the more expensive stores—she may even argue that in the long run such stores are more economical than other places with lower prices. She *must* be seen with the right people in the right places. Perhaps above all, her code prevents her from giving an impression to business associates, neighbors, or others that she cannot afford the luxuries or comforts she thinks a person of her social class should have. To some extent, therefore, she is living a life of deception.

But she is deceiving herself most of all. She does so, I think, because she fears that people will somehow think less of her if she admits openly that, in her financial condition, constant changes in dress styles are too much for her to keep up with, that she really cannot afford an expensive address, or that it strains her budget to entertain on a lavish scale. Of course, she is a victim of the age-old temptation, which exists on all levels of society, to "keep up with the Joneses."

This urge to live—or to seem to live—as well as or better than our neighbors is difficult to resist. There seems to be a universal tendency to desire to give others the impression that we have a larger income than we really do and that we can afford, without pain, all of the things that everyone else has.

It takes a particular kind of determination to be able to say (to yourself, at least) that you won't engage in a race to show your business associates and neighbors how well-off you are and to admit honestly that your income does not permit you the luxuries others may seem able to afford. Once you take this step, however, the road to financial contentment becomes surprisingly smoother.

I once suggested to the debt-ridden young parents of three children that their point of view had to change from one of worry about what their neighbors thought, to one of concern solely for whether they really needed the things they were tempted to buy. Of course, one cannot change habits of a lifetime overnight. It took a long time for this couple to convince themselves that their neighbors would not take up a collection to send their children to college, to support them in their old age, or to buy any of the other things they wanted in the future. Gradually, they came to realize that their financial destiny lay only in their own hands and that by worrying about what their neighbors thought, they were, in a way, letting them dictate what they themselves should do with their own income.

"When we finally came to care less about what our neighbors might say about our spending habits, we found it easy to do things that would have terrified us before," they told me several years later. Instead of buying a new car every two years to impress the neighbors, they decided to hold on to their old one for as long as it would run. The wife had formerly bought her children's clothes at one of the best shops in her community. Then she decided to frequent some of the thrift shops around town and found excellent used clothing for her children, herself, and even her husband, at a small fraction of their original cost. She and her husband decided that even if their richer neighbors down the road didn't like it, they would get out their old ladder and paint the outside of their house by themselves. Instead of taking a summer cottage at an expensive resort, they bought a used camper, mounted it on a pickup truck, and drove off on a "do it yourself" vacation, to save motel and restaurant bills.

"Once we got into the habit of thinking about economical ways of doing things," the wife said, "it became a game with us. Once, I would have died on the spot if a neighbor saw me enter a bakery store where they sold day-old bread at half the regular price. Now I shop at the store a couple of times a month, buy enough bread for a couple of weeks, and keep it in my freezer. When we heat it, it tastes as if it had just come from the bakery. I really enjoy money-saving tricks of that kind.

"Most important of all, we have discovered something I was completely blind to before. When we were spending money faster than it came in, we thought we had to live on a certain scale to impress the richer people in the community. To our surprise, we discovered that people who are well-off are often a lot sharper in practicing the money-saving tricks that we learned."

At this point, many readers doubtless have concluded that such a Spartan existence is not for them. If they must choose between penny-pinching and living "the good life," they will take the latter, even if it means remaining in debt. Of course, I do not recommend that people give up their important pleasures for the sake of a few extra dollars in the bank. One of my fundamental beliefs is that money was made to be used. I do not advocate that anyone enter the competition to become the richest person in the cemetery.

I do propose, however, that you make a decision to use your income in the way that most effectively fits your plans. If you want to spend it all on payday and live on beans the rest of the week, that's fine with me. I ask only that you recognize that it is not possible for you to live to the hilt on payday and have filet mignon every other night as well. This book is addressed primarily to people who want to handle their incomes so that they can have the comforts of life along the way and so that when they are ready to retire, they will have no regrets about the things they cannot do because they have let so much money slip through their fingers. I am trying to help readers who are ready to learn how to make the hard choice to do without some things today in order to be able to "do with" tomorrow and who do not think that the government will do everything for them or that Social Security is all they will need.

But being able to "do with" tomorrow does not mean you must move into a cold-water flat and forego life's present comforts. I consider such a philosophy inappropriate—as unwarranted as the idea that you should never give a thought to the future. Both ideas are extreme. Our economy and way of living are so set up that a person can have most of the good things he wants without paying through the nose for them. You can have a pleasant time at a back-yard picnic eating hamburgers at perhaps one-tenth the cost of a garden party at which champagne and steaks are served by butlers. When you take a trip, you can get from here to there without much additional inconvenience by driving a three-year-old car that is in good shape instead of one fresh from the showroom. If you shop around, you can find appliances and other necessities for your home for several dollars less than they cost in the high-rent district. You can buy clothing at sales for considerably less than they cost at other times.

Being a careful money manager does not mean living in rigid simplicity or dullness. If you develop the knowledge and experience necessary to get the maximum effectiveness from your money—whether you are earning, spending, saving, or investing it—you will find that it becomes an enjoyable game. Your only opponent will be yourself. In this game, you will be surprised to discover how few comforts you will have to forego and how pleasurable it is to get more out of your income than others are getting out of theirs. Your future will become brighter, your horizons broader, and your entire life happier.

ONE Handling Money Is Everybody's Job

"Why is it necessary to teach everybody how to use money effectively? Isn't it up to husbands and fathers to provide for their families and accept the responsibility of handling all the important money matters?"

When I started teaching the facts of financial life more than thirty years ago, this question was more common than it is today. Bankers, investment men, business executives, and, above all, the typical male often questioned the need and wisdom of making women and children financially intelligent. Some men considered the subject too sacred even to discuss in front of their wives and offspring. Many told their wives: "Why bother your pretty little head about these mundane things? Just keep sweet and lovely, and we'll handle the rest." Male newspaper columnists painted a grotesque picture of women investing in a corporation because they favored the color of the stock certificates it issued, were taken in by the corporation's gallant executive, or liked the way its board chairman furnished his home.

Most men seemed to think that women were unable to understand and in fact did not care to learn the details of high finance and that the task of balancing a checkbook would throw the typical female into a panic. Many women also believed this. But the conditions of modern life make it necessary for everyone

—man, woman, and child—to understand how to use the all-important tool of money.

Ten years ago, a woman told me, "I don't know the difference between a stock and a bond, and I never want to know. My husband handles everything. That is as nature intended it to be—man should be the brains of the house and woman the heart." A few years later, her husband suffered a heart attack, and she faced the problem of trying to decide what to do with the various pieces of stock and real estate he owned. Part of the estate consisted of a collection of odds and ends apparently bought for no reason and often in the most expensive ways—eighteen shares of this, twenty-three shares of something else, eighty shares of a company that had gone out of business, their winter and summer homes, and so on. If anything was needed to debunk the theory that men are naturally superior to women in handling financial affairs, this was it. This widow had to learn how to manage her affairs in a hurry. Once she was able to rid herself of the myth that women were not equipped to deal with such matters, she did a marvelous job and actually achieved better returns from her investments than her husband ever did.

"Isn't money management too much for the average woman? After all, she has never had training in such matters."

I like to think that the results achieved by the many thousands of women attending my Finance Forum courses have helped make it plain to everyone that neither sex has a monopoly on brains and the ability to use them. Today, more than ever, women have had to learn how to handle their own financial affairs. For example, while today's widow wisely seeks expert advice in the settling of her husband's estate and the investment of funds, she also usually wants to know what is going on. No longer is it considered "ladylike" for a woman to turn her affairs over to someone else and never question what is being done with her money. Millions of women now have incomes of their own—and it is no longer the "proper" thing for them to avoid "soiling" their dainty hands at a job that produces income. Today's typical girl expects to work after she finishes her schooling, for a while after marriage, perhaps part-time while her children are young, and again when her children are grown. The modern girl who earns an income wants, rightly, to have something to say about how it is used. Even wives who never work outside the home have much greater influence over the way the family's income is spent and invested than they did thirty years ago.

"On your radio program, you said that women made the country's financial wheels go 'round. What is your evidence for this?"

According to conservative estimates by the General Federation of Women's Clubs, of every $5.00 paid out in wages and salaries in the United States, more than $1.00 finds its way directly into the purses of American women. But of every $5.00 spent, $4.00 is directly laid out by women.

In a majority of cases, women maintain the joint checking accounts in their families. Studies by the Institute of Life Insurance show that the majority of checks written in joint husband-wife accounts bear the wife's signature.

"What do women buy directly and indirectly for their families, and how influential are they in deciding the fate of American business?"

While it is not news that women are responsible for the purchase of their own and their children's clothing, research studies by Marketing Survey Associates show that wives exert a surprising influence on the clothes their husbands wear. They often buy their husbands' shirts, socks, and ties themselves, and they often go with them as they shop for a new suit or hat. It seems to be a rare husband who will buy an article of clothing of which his wife disapproves. When a wife does not accompany her husband, she often reveals her preferences in advance, telling him he looks handsome in a blue suit or does not appear to his best advantage in pin stripes.

As sales executives realize, women exert a direct or indirect influence over every major item the typical family buys. Advertising agency spokesmen, quoted in the *New York Times*, say that women generally decide the style and color of the family automobile, while the husband's decision governs the mechanical parts alone. Women almost always decide what kind of refrigerator, washing machine, dryer, and electric dishwasher the family will have and almost single-handedly choose the soap powder, detergents, toothpaste, and other toiletries used in the home.

In his book, *The Impact of Women*, Henry S. Galus states that the female image even permeates advertising for products intended for males. If a product is intended for both men and women, advertisers often try to reach the women. The construction, style, color, and accessory conveniences of products that customarily concern husbands are slanted to impress wives, for advertisers know that if the wife is "sold," she will badger her husband into buying. For instance, a few years ago manufacturers of pleasure boats offered only a choice of blue or green colors. Today, according to boating magazines, the manufacturer who wants to sell his craft must make certain that the galley is convenient, serviceable, and attractive. Unless the wife is sold on the convenience and attractiveness of the area in which food will be cooked and served—as well as on the boat's overall appearance—many sales will be lost. The rapid rise in recent years in sales of outdoor tent trailers and "pickup campers," in which trailers are mounted on trucks, is attributed almost entirely to women's influence—their desire to go camping without the discomfort and feeling of insecurity they experience sleeping on the ground.

The great influence of the woman extends to just about everything the family spends its money on. She is the one who must be satisfied that the home fits the family's needs as she sees them. She determines what kind of furniture they will have, what schools the children will attend, where they will spend their vacation, how they will use their recreation money. She will have a great deal to say—and, in increasing numbers of cases, the real power to decide—about how much of their income the family will save, what the money will be saved for, and where it will be saved. She may decide how much insurance she and her family will carry.

No longer is a woman accused of infringing upon the male's preserve when she takes an active interest in family money matters. No longer does she think that the male is particularly endowed, by some act of nature, with the ability to understand these problems, while she is not. The fact is that men are not "naturally" better at figures than women. The modern girl has sat next to boys in school and college; she knows that a female can be just as adept at adding, subtracting, multiplying, and dividing as her male counterpart, and that she is just as capable of putting her common sense to work in the solution of monetary problems.

The idea that women are not equipped to "bother their pretty heads" about even the more difficult questions of international finance, for instance, the workings of such institutions as the International Monetary Bank or Federal Reserve System, is also going by the board. Although some major stock exchanges still bar women members, few of their officers would want to argue that women cannot hold their own in a battle of wits with men. Since I pioneered in the field of investment counseling, I have seen women entering the counseling ranks in every part of the nation. We have nationally known women commentators on international affairs. Some highly regarded professors on the subject of money management at the nation's universities are women. Women are running banks and sitting on the boards of directors of insurance companies and other great financial institutions.

When I lecture before mixed groups, I usually find the women in the audience at least as perceptive and attentive as the men, and often more so. The typical modern wife knows a great deal more than her husband about the intricacies of shopping, of using credit wisely, of getting the maximum benefit and income from savings, of avoiding the pitfalls of gyps and rackets—in sum, of making dollars travel further and do a more effective job. Their questions indicate a good understanding of financial processes.

"Do you think the majority of women really want to learn about money management?"

When, occasionally, I meet a woman who says that she does not know anything about such matters as buying insurance, making wills, using credit, or figuring interest rates, I am forced to conclude that she has been brainwashed into thinking that it detracts from her delicate femininity if she knows about these things. This is not so. Anyone with even an elementary school education, anyone who can add and subtract and use the simple multiplication table, anyone who has a real desire to make effective use of this all-important tool, can be an effective money handler and completely feminine as well.

"You don't seem to leave much room for husbands. Do you think men should forget about this subject and leave it to their wives?"

Not at all! There are many important areas men must understand in order to protect a family's financial future. They should educate themselves about such essential matters as saving and investing, avoiding the unwise use of credit and the excessive costs of it, making the right insurance decisions, getting the most for their housing dollar, understanding the basic ins and outs of the income tax laws so that they do not pay more to the government than is legally due. And children—both girls and boys—must learn about money management so that they will be properly equipped when they accept responsibilities as wives and husbands. This subject is so broad and so vital that I'll repeat what I said at the beginning: it's a job for everyone.

"What is the first requirement for anyone who hopes to be competent about money?"

My first rule is to keep all important papers in one place—to know what their provisions are and where they are so that you (or someone else) can get to them easily in an emergency. The second requirement is to know exactly what you are spending your money on. At this point, I will discuss what papers you should keep together; we will get to the matter of putting your spending patterns down on paper later.

Many persons who are remarkably competent and efficient in most aspects of their professional and personal lives are incredibly sloppy when it comes to simple financial record-keeping. More people than I care to think about would be shocked at the idea of managing any business operation under a hat, yet they deal with their own personal affairs in that way.

Being sloppy in financial record-keeping—for instance, scattering important papers all over the place—usually has no disastrous consequences as long as someone alive and present knows where the papers are. But in an extreme emergency—death, serious accident, absence for prolonged periods—someone who must get the papers but does not know where they are may have to pay a high price in time and money to assemble them.

Whether you are single or married, you should keep all of the important financial papers for yourself and your family in one place. If you are single, your attorney and your next of kin (parents, brothers or sisters, children, or others close to you) should at least know where these papers can be obtained. You may not want everyone to know all of the details of your financial life—how much you are worth, how much insurance you carry, the details of your will—and you can keep such information private by keeping the papers dealing with them in a safe place. But someone in whom you have confidence should be told that this material is available there in the event of your death or complete disability.

If you are married and are responsible for handling your family's financial records, you should list all important information—the name of the lawyer who has your will, location and number of safe deposit box, types and numbers of insurance policies, names of insurance companies and agents, and other vital information I shall detail in the following pages. Make certain that your marriage partner knows where this list is kept.

The partner who handles such matters should keep all of the valuable papers and records in one safe place and should tell the other where that safe place is. Untold tension, difficulty, hardship, and irritation can be avoided when this is done.

"What papers should we have in one place?"

Your last will in effect—the one that supersedes all previous wills.

Deeds, mortgages, bills of sale, etc., of all the major property you own; for example, if you own a home, the price you paid for it, its lot and block number on the community tax rolls, the existence of any mortgage on your property, the name and address of the mortgage holder, the amount outstanding, and the name and address of the lawyer who negotiated its purchase.

A record of all savings and investments—the number of savings accounts at any savings institutions, the exact names of the account holders, and details of where the necessary bankbooks can be found.

Papers confirming your participation in any profit-sharing or pension plans of your employers, such as receipts, deposits, statements of your equity, etc.

All your stocks and bonds, or a complete record of them including their exact certificate numbers. You should retain brokers' statements verifying the date and price paid when securities were bought and the date and price received when they were sold. These records may be necessary not only to settle your estate but also for your own tax purposes. If you do not have the actual stocks and bonds in your possession, you should list where your securities are held and also the names and addresses of your investment brokers, counselors, banks, or others who might have records of your transactions.

A record of all loans—money owed to you by others and money you yourself owe. In one case, a husband loaned his brother $15,000 to help him start a restaurant. The loan was "sealed" with a handshake, and the husband neglected to record it. He died suddenly of a heart attack, and his widow did not even know of the loan. Of course, she had no legal right to ask her brother-in-law to repay it. Fortunately, he was an honorable man, and he repaid it promptly. In this case, the widow did not lose out, but she could just as easily have been unable to collect the amount because of the absence of any written agreement and any indication of the existence of the loan.

All pertinent details covering other items of personal property. Bills of sale for all of your major purchases—automobile, furniture, appliances, expensive articles of clothing such as furs or jewelry—will be useful to have if you wish to sell any of these items later; if they are damaged, destroyed, or stolen, and you seek to recover the amount of loss from your insurance company; and also for the purpose of valuing an estate in the event of death.

All vital insurance papers—life, fire, personal liability, health and accident, and other policies. From such policies it should be easy to ascertain amounts of coverage, numbers of policies in force, and the names and addresses of the insurance companies involved and of your local insurance broker. Also remember that even small business firms often have life and health insurance policies on employees—sometimes, strange to say, without the employees' even knowing about them.

Important personal papers. One of your valuable possessions is the equity you have built up in Social Security insurance. Almost everyone who has worked for someone else, as well as most self-employed persons, has made Social Security payments and has been issued a numbered Social Security card. These contributions, as well as those the law requires employers to make, total hundreds of dollars a year and add up to a substantial amount, which may accrue to you upon your retirement or to your heirs upon your death. There are so many names in the Social Security master files in Baltimore that your name is almost surely duplicated, and the one thing that identifies you positively and enables your claim to be expedited is your Social

Security number. It is important to keep your card and a record of your number in a safe place. Also keep a duplicate list of your credit cards and their numbers so that you will be able to report them in the event they are lost or stolen.

It is also worthwhile to make a list of all employers with whom you have worked, along with the dates of employment and salary earned. This record enables you to check on the amounts contributed to the Social Security headquarters in your name and to make sure that no credit has gone astray or been credited to different accounts.

You should also keep under lock and key all personal papers you may need to prove your identity or status—such as birth certificates, marriage licenses, and passports. Remember, too, that you may be called upon, years from now, to confirm the figures you have put on this year's income tax papers, so you should keep all tax records seven years.

"Where should our important papers be kept? We now have them all in a desk drawer, where they are easy to get at."

As far as most people are concerned, there is only one answer to this question: all of your important documents and valuables should be kept in a safe deposit box in a bank. It is safe. It is private—no one has access to it except you (and your spouse, if you are married and hold the box jointly). Finally, it is inexpensive—a small one can be rented for about $6.00 a year.

The privacy of your safe deposit box is ensured by the fact that keys are given only to those in whose names it is issued. As an added precaution, the bank also has a key. Both keys must be used to open the box. A person authorized to use the box must have a key and must identify himself. This reduces the chance that someone who found or stole your key would be able to open your box. However, because the banks seal safe deposit boxes upon the death of the box-holder, I recommend that certain valuables be kept outside the box—your will, for instance, and the deed to your cemetery plot. A court order may be needed to authorize the bank to open the box for your survivors; the cemetery deed will at least enable them to go ahead with the funeral and burial services.

I do not recommend keeping valuable papers at home in desk drawers, strong boxes, or home safes. It is all too easy for someone to break them open or walk off with them. In fact, I cannot think of a stronger inducement to a burglar than the sight of a safe in a private home. It immediately suggests that valuables are kept inside, and it would probably be the first item he would try to open or take away with him.

"How important is it to have a will? We don't have enough to make a will seem worthwhile."

You owe it to yourself to keep your important papers together, and you also owe it to those you leave behind when you die to save them untold trouble and hardship. The way to save them unneeded difficulty is to leave a will. This is a necessity for any man or woman, married or single.

You may think, as many people do, that making a will is an involved process that takes a great amount of time, requires a detailed listing of all your possessions, and is suitable only for the wealthy. Let me repeat: even if your assets total no more than a few hundred dollars—in the form of clothing, jewelry, furniture, household appliances, or an automobile—you should hire a lawyer to draw up a legal statement that will state specifically whom you want to have your possessions upon your death.

"Suppose I die without leaving a will. What could happen?"

Books have been written about the consequences of the deaths of persons who did not leave clear statements of their intentions behind them. Long and complicated legal battles have taken place among heirs or supposed heirs—among children, brothers and sisters, parents and children, cousins, aunts, uncles, second and third cousins, and even more distant relatives—all claiming some share of a deceased person's estate. These cases don't necessarily involve a lot of money. For instance, three children went to court battling each other for possession of their father's gold watch, something with no great monetary value but great sentimental significance. The children were unable to settle the dispute amicably, and once their emotions got into play, they lost all sense of proportion. They became willing to spend thousands of dollars over an object worth less than $100.

The reason everyone should make a will is that it is incorrect to assume that your closest relatives (for example, your children) will automatically inherit everything if there are no other instructions. The laws of the different states vary on this point, and indeed on many other aspects of inheritance, so that if you die without making a will you may in effect be letting the legislature of your state decide who should get your property. It is true that in most cases, when a parent dies, the surviving children are legally entitled to shares of the estate. Even under these circumstances, however, the law may require the court to appoint a guardian or executor to protect the children's interests, if they are under age, and a stranger may then determine how and when they are to receive their share. Of course, the guardian has to be paid out of the same money.

If you are married and have minor children and your marriage partner dies without leaving a will, you may discover that your children are his legal heirs as well as you—and that before you can spend any of the estate money on their behalf, even for food, clothing, shelter, and education, you need the approval of someone designated by the court. If your children are grown up and well able to support themselves, they may still share in your partner's estate even if it means you will not get enough to live comfortably.

"Why don't people make wills?"

There are several common reasons, none of which, in my opinion, is valid. Some people, particularly young ones, don't think death can happen to them. Others, of all ages, don't want to think about it, as though they can eliminate it by refusing to consider it. Of course, death strikes at all ages. You need only pick up a newspaper to read of deaths in automobile accidents, plane crashes, and even from heart attacks happening to persons in the prime of life. The possibility of sudden death is ever present, regardless of one's age.

A second objection is that making a will is too involved and that people don't have time to bother with it. Those who believe this sometimes think that they must make an inventory of every knife and fork they own. This is not so. All you need to do is make a written statement declaring whom you want to give your possessions to. If you want a particular person to have special possessions—for instance, a favorite cousin to have your silver or dishes—you need only make such bequests specifically.

Some think that a will, once made, is binding for all time. Also, some believe that after making a will they will not be able to sell any of their property or change heirs if they want to. Neither of these beliefs is true. You can change your will as often as you wish. A will does not become final and irrevocable until your death, and only the last one that you have properly made is considered binding. This means that you can make changes as conditions change; as some of your children cease to be minors, for example, you might want them to have a lesser share of your estate so that more will be left for the education of those still under twenty-one.

"I want to leave some money to one nephew but not to another, because he'll go right out and waste it. If I make a will, will it be possible to keep the second nephew from knowing about it? I don't want him to get angry with me."

The elderly woman who asked this question was expressing another common mistake about wills. No one except your lawyer (who is sworn to secrecy) need know that you have made a will or what it says. Its provisions can be kept secret and made public only after your death.

Perhaps the most common reason people fail to make wills is that they fear it will be a costly, time-consuming process and that a lawyer may not want to be bothered with drawing up a "cheap one." The fact is that an ordinary will rarely costs more than $50.00 to $100 to set up, including interviews with the lawyer, typing the will, and obtaining the signatures of witnesses testifying that you indeed signed the document and knew what you were doing when you signed it.

"What do you think of the idea of my drawing up my own will? It seems to me that I could save a lot of money that way."

It is true that if you make a clear statement of your intentions of how you want to dispose of your property and have it witnessed by two persons, it can be accepted as a legal document. Few persons, however, know all of the ins and outs of the laws of their state and the various tax angles, and if a will fails to meet certain legal requirements or fails to recognize the legal rights of heirs; it may be thrown out altogether or substantially changed by a court. If your language is not precise, the result may be a host of lawsuits. Nor is the amount of your estate any guarantee that there will not be suits. People are always going to court and fighting to the last ditch, not for money, but for "the principle of the thing."

As a common rule, a husband or wife is automatically entitled, by law, to a third of the partner's estate. If a will does not bequeath this amount to him or her, he or she can go to court and have the will broken unless there has been an agreement to the contrary made before the marriage. Men and women marrying late in life should remember this. It is possible to make a premarital agreement (which a lawyer should prepare) by which the new husband or wife relinquishes the legal rights. This is a handy device to protect yourself against someone you think may be marrying you for your money. If you want to do so, you can tear up this premarital agreement any time after marriage.

The advice I give everyone is to get a qualified lawyer who specializes in probating (legally proving the validity of) estates. Such a lawyer has had experience in drawing up wills and knows the laws of your state. When he draws up your will for you, you will have the security of knowing that there will be no battling over your real intentions. If you move to another state, you should have your will reviewed by a competent attorney in the new state to make sure that it conforms to that state's requirements.

Lawyers often have members of their own staff witness the wills they draw up. The lawyers usually keep in touch with these witnesses thereafter, because the witnesses will have to testify after the will is entered for probate that they were indeed present when you signed the document.

"Where should I keep the signed copy of my will?"

It is wise to leave your signed will with the lawyer who draws it up for you. He will then be ready to execute it upon death. As I have mentioned, I do not advise keeping it in your safe deposit box, because banks customarily seal these boxes after the death of the box-holder and do not release the contents until they know who is legally entitled to them. If your will is in the box, your survivors might have to obtain a court order to get it out. Again, don't forget to keep, in a convenient place, a list showing where your important papers are. In fact, it is wise to keep copies of this in several places. This list should include the name and address of the lawyer who has the master copy of your will.

TWO What Does Your Financial X Ray Reveal?

"What do I have to do to be a 'good money manager'? As things stand now, I never seem to know where my money goes."

Before you can begin to manage your financial affairs in a satisfactory way, it is essential that you know exactly how you stand financially: how much you are really worth, how much you are earning, how much you are spending, what you are spending it on, how much you are saving, and how you are investing. Without these basic facts, you will continually operate in the dark and will be unable to make intelligent and effective decisions.

In order to get these facts, it is necessary to take what I call a financial X ray. This financial X ray is a thorough examination, something like the physical examination a physician gives you in a comprehensive checkup. After such an examination, the physician can tell you what condition you are in and prescribe a course of action to keep you in, or get you back to, good health. Similarly, a financial X ray gets to the true state of your economic condition. With the results of your financial X ray, I can prescribe a financial program specifically suited to your needs.

Before you dismiss this idea by commenting that you already know all about your finances, let me say that over the years I have met few people who can make even a close estimate of their actual worth. Of course, you don't need a balance sheet to tell you whether you can afford a yacht or even whether you have enough cash on hand or in the bank to buy a new pair of shoes. But if you are like the average person, you will be off the mark by as much as $1,000 or more as to your total overall worth today unless you have taken the trouble to make a study of your real condition.

The report of a financial X ray is like the balance sheet corporations issue to their stockholders every year. On one side of the sheet they list all of their assets and on the other side their liabilities. In the same way, your financial report can closely determine how much actual cash could be obtained if you died and your heirs had to sell all you own or if you yourself wanted to dispose of all your possessions.

When you make this careful appraisal, you may find that you are worth a great deal more than you think you are—or perhaps a great deal less. One woman "buys" a great number of things on the installment plan. She then considers that she owns them, completely disregarding the amount she still owes and will have to pay on them if the sellers are not to take them away from her. She has a lovely home, lovely furniture, a new car, and fine clothes. She regards herself as well-off; actually, she owes many thousands of dollars on all these things, and if she had to sell them, she could not get as much as she owes. She is running deeper and deeper into debt, but she does not realize it.

"What should I list on my personal financial statement to give me an accurate picture of my current worth?"

On one side, you should note your assets: those items to which you hold title or which are in your possession. This would include:

Your cash and "cash equivalents." All you have on hand as well as your holdings in banks and savings institutions—the current amount you have in savings and loan companies or savings banks, checking accounts, or trust funds.

All your bonds (including government savings bonds). Their value is what you could realize for them today.

Cash value of all insurance policies. If you have held life insurance policies other than term insurance for any period of time, you have probably paid more than the cost of the actual insurance itself. The extra amount goes into the "cash surrender value" and is the amount the insurance company would pay you if you no longer wished to carry the policy.

Cash value in pension plans. Many employers set up special plans for their employees and regularly contribute funds to be disbursed when employees retire. Some employers put in a certain amount each pay period if the employee also puts in a certain amount; in other cases, the employer makes the entire contribution. Whenever an employee has made contributions, he can withdraw from the plan and take his money out when he chooses, but he may not be able to rejoin the pension plan later. On the other hand, if all the contributions have been made by his employer, he may not be entitled to receive anything if he quits his job. Because individual pension plans vary so much, an employee should learn the exact provisions of the particular employer's plan and determine what, if anything, he could get if he were to withdraw from the plan today. Some employees have equities in pensions amounting to thousands of dollars—a sum large enough to play an important part in any financial decisions they make.

Value of real estate owned. Under assets, list what you believe you could sell your properties for—house, lots, business properties, etc.—less any commissions and taxes you would have to pay. For example, if you bought a lot ten years ago for $10,000 and you are sure you could sell it through a broker for $20,000, you would list its present value not at $20,000 but at that amount minus a broker's commission, which might run about 5 or 6 per cent, and the capital gains taxes on your profit. Capital gains tax is one-half that of your normal income tax and in no event more than 25 per cent of your profit.

If the tax on your gain figured as normal income would be 30 per cent, the capital gain rate would be 15 per cent, or $1,450 on your net profit of about $9,000. Thus your real estate ownership would be shown on your balance sheet, not at $20,000, but, more realistically, at $17,550. (On this side of your financial statement, you do not list amounts outstanding against you, such as mortgages or other loans. You make this notation on the other side of your statement, under liabilities, which will then be subtracted from your total assets.)

All shares in stocks, mutual funds, private businesses, or other operations. If you own a private business in whole or in part, list its value as it would be if it were sold today, less any applicable taxes. If you own common stocks or mutual funds, list the amounts at which they could be liquidated as of now, less taxes. The market price is the "bid" price quoted in the published stock tables or by your broker. It is the price buyers are willing to pay at this time.

All loans owed to you that you have reasonable prospects of collecting. There is no point in including among your assets, for example, the few hundred dollars you loaned some years ago to a friend you have not heard from since. Such loans should be written off as bad debts.

All your personal property. In this area particularly, most people tend to underestimate the total value of their holdings. Over the years, you have probably accumulated possessions that cost thousands of dollars when they were new. While they may be worth only a fraction of their former value now, you might nevertheless get a sizable amount for them if you sold them all.

Of course, you don't have to try to determine the worth of every knife and fork you own. However, if you have insurance (as you should) to cover the loss of your personal property through damage, theft, or fire, you should have some kind of list of the major possessions, including bills of sale if possible, or, in any event, a notation of the date purchased, the price paid, and the name of the seller. Such a list might include all items costing more than $100 when new. Thus it would include your automobile, large pieces of furniture, high-fidelity equipment, silverware, dishes, furs, diamonds and important jewelry, and also your television set. (Furs, jewelry, and television sets seem to be the items most often taken when a house is burglarized. If they are stolen, the bills of sale will enable you to collect more readily from your insurance company.)

The current value of your automobile can be obtained easily. You need only consult the "autos for sale" classified advertising section of your daily newspaper and determine what other cars of the same model, year, and equipment are selling for. Remember, however, that if you sell to a used car dealer you probably will not get more than 80 per cent of the going retail price. While diamonds and other jewelry may be worth more today than when you bought them, most personal possessions depreciate in value quickly. A living room set for which you paid in excess of $1,000 a few years ago might be worth only $100 if you wanted to sell it now. Used dresses, shoes, hats, coats, etc., are rarely worth more than 15 per cent of their original value.

When you have listed your assets, add up the total. You will probably be surprised to note its size; it may well run to thousands of dollars. However, this does not give you the total picture of your financial condition. We must now consider the amounts of money you owe or will be responsible for paying—your liabilities.

"What do you mean by 'liabilities'? What should my list of them include?"

Most persons have at least a few debts, even if the bills have not yet been presented to them. These debts are your liabilities. Your list of them might include:

All charge accounts. Goods or services you have purchased for which you have not yet paid.

Utility bills. Amounts you now owe your phone, gas and electric, and water companies for services already provided, which you have not yet been asked to pay. (Some utilities require customers to post a deposit when this service is begun. These deposits should be listed among your assets. It may be that your deposits are greater than the amounts you owe at any given time.)

Amounts owed to doctors and dentists and for other medical and dental services.

All loans outstanding. Most important of these might be any mortgages on your home or other property—the amounts you would have to pay if you wanted to own the property free and clear. Other loans might be collateral on stocks or bonds—the amounts a bank or other lending institution has advanced you against securities you have given them to hold; loans made against the cash value of your insurance policy or savings bank passbook; installment loans, including total amounts you still owe on your automobile or anything else bought on a time-payment plan and on loans for home improvements or other personal needs.

All taxes now due. If you are employed, certain sums have probably been deducted from your income each month to keep you on a "pay as you go" basis. But perhaps you have had other income during the year, on which taxes have not been collected. For example, if you have sold stocks, bonds, real estate, or other property at a profit, you may owe the government a capital gains tax if you held the property more than six months or a regular tax if you held it less than six months.

Any other debts outstanding.

"What is 'net worth,' and how can I tell what mine is?"

Total all your liabilities, subtract your total liabilities from your total assets, and the result is your net worth: approximately the cash you would have if you were to sell all you own, pay all your debts, and strip to your bare bones.

Your net worth is what you are actually worth here and now. Many people find it a revelation. As I have mentioned, some who "own" many luxurious items and have a large take-home pay consider themselves well-off, yet they discover that their debts are far greater than they have ever imagined. Equally often, people who think that they have not made any substantial economic progress over the years are astonished to discover how much they are really worth. Amounts they have almost never thought about are hidden away in the form of pension plans, cash values of insurance, and real and personal property.

Only with a personal financial statement, therefore, can you really tell what you can and cannot afford to buy. Because this statement tells you whether you are rich or poor, well-to-do or living on the brink of insolvency, it is something you must know in order to operate intelligently on a day-by-day basis.

"How important is it to know how much I really spend on various items?"

To get an X ray of your financial health, you must know what you are doing with your money. Are you spending more than you earn, saving out of your income, or closely matching your outgo to your income? You may think you know the answer, but do not be too sure. The fact is that most people do not know clearly, for what they are saving or spending may be somewhat hidden. For example, they may forget that the monthly payment they make to the lending institution holding their mortgage includes a payment to reduce the principal they owe, thereby increasing their equity in their home. They may not realize that the cash value of their share in their company's pension plan is increasing rapidly. If they own stocks or mutual funds, they may not realize the extent to which the value of their holdings is increasing.

On the other hand, many persons running into debt more heavily every year are not aware of it. The "buy now and pay later" opportunities that exist everywhere make this easier to do than most people imagine. It is amazingly simple to look at the contract for a new automobile as just monthly payments of $100 or so per month for thirty-six months. The $100 may seem like a small amount, yet you are adding to your outstanding debt by thousands of dollars. Some people sell shares of stock at a profit and think they have gained more than they really have. One man sold some stock at a profit of $3,000. He decided to spend all the gains by taking his wife on a vacation to Hawaii. He returned home thinking that he was even financially, but he had overlooked the fact that he would have to pay $700 in taxes on his gains.

"How do I determine whether my income is greater than my outgo or vice versa?"

The best way I know of is to make an itemized account of all the money you take in during a specified period—every month, preferably—and the amounts you must pay out to meet expenses in that period. Many of your expenses are fixed; they vary little, if at all, from month to month. Others are adjustable and can be raised or lowered, depending upon your desires.

In suggesting to my students at The Finance Forum of America that they make a careful study of their income and outgo, I urge them first to estimate their annual intake—all the money they either have received or will receive during the year. I then suggest that they divide this total amount by twelve to arrive at the corresponding monthly figure.

Most people's annual income consists most importantly of salary or wages. (This should be the gross salary—the amount the employer pays you *before* he makes any deductions for taxes, Social Security, group insurance plans, unemployment insurance, pension plans, or other purposes.) Of course, if you are married and you and your spouse both have incomes, both should be included.

Remember to include all income from any other sources, even though you may not receive it directly. This might consist of income from rents or royalties, interest or dividends on savings or investments, payments you receive under annuity, pension, or trust arrangements, or amounts credited to you in accounts you could put your hands on if you wanted to.

This total annual income is not only what you get this year, it is also what you can reasonably count on every year. It does not include "paper" gains on investments—increases in the value of stock you have not sold, for example. Incidentally, gains or losses from the sale of investments in any year usually are described as "nonrecurring income"—the kind it is not prudent to count on as a continuing thing.

Your next step is to determine how much money is flowing out each year and where it is going. List your fixed expenses, including the following:

Housing cost. If you rent a house or apartment, this is the monthly rent you pay. If you own your own place, it is the amount you must pay in taxes, interest charges on a mortgage if you have one, and necessary repairs and maintenance of the house structure itself. As a rule of thumb, one housing expert suggests that for such things as painting the exterior, replacing roof shingles, and installing a new furnace, it costs about 1 to 2 per cent of the value of the house each year, depending on its age.

Household maintenance charges. These include costs of heating, electricity, gas and water, interior decorating, etc. Such costs vary from month to month, particularly for heat, so the best thing is to compute their cost on an annual basis and divide by twelve to arrive at the average monthly figure. If you have maintenance services for your home—for example, a gardener who cares for your lawn and yard, a handyman, or other household help—their costs should also be tallied on the basis of an average monthly figure.

Insurance premiums. This cost might be broken down to account for the different kinds of insurance you carry. For instance, there is insurance by homeowners on the building itself. Premiums on this insurance are sometimes included in payments to the lending institution holding the mortgage on your home, and you may already have made allowances for it in the section dealing with your monthly mortgage payment. Other payments include automobile insurance, personal property insurance (the kind covering all household effects, which entitles you to recovery in case they are lost, damaged, or destroyed as a result of fire or other specified conditions); and personal liability insurance (the kind covering you against damages you or members of your family and household may inflict upon other persons). Most times, all of these are combined into what is called a homeowner's or tenant's policy. Other insurance policies are life, accident, health, hospitalization, and major medical.

Taxes. If you have a home mortgage and are making monthly payments to a mortgage lender, these may include a sum for taxes. If such taxes have already been included in the category of housing expenses, naturally you do not include them here. Taxes you pay directly should, however, be included.

Your federal income taxes should be listed here, even if your employer pays them out of your salary. Your Social Security and unemployment insurance taxes also should be tabulated here. When you compute all the taxes you pay, you may be shocked at the total amount you see. When taxes are taken directly out of an individual's salary, he often is not aware of how much work he must do for the services his government gives him.

Education. Cost of tuition, books, etc., for yourself, spouse, or children.

These fixed expenditures should now be totaled. There is not much you can do about them, at least over the short term.

I'm sure you can think of many expenses that are somewhat easier for you to cut down on, at least over the short term. Such items of expense might include:

Food and other items used in the ordinary maintenance of your household. Groceries, meat and fish, milk and other dairy products, as well as soaps, soap powders, light bulbs, and the like.

Clothes. Coats, suits, dresses, blouses, undergarments, hats, footwear, hosiery, accessories. Include also the cost of cleaning and repairing these items. Many people underestimate somewhat the amounts spent in this area.

Personal care and health. List how much is spent at the barber or beauty shop each month, your average dental and medical bills figured on a monthly basis, and the cost of prescription drugs, vitamins, cosmetics, toilet articles, and similar items—eyeglasses, eye examinations, etc.

Transportation. The biggest item in this category probably relates to car costs—your cost for gas, oil, periodic lubrication jobs, and checkups, as well as normal wear and tear, such as replacement of tires every thirty thousand miles or so. In this connection, studies by the American Automobile Association suggest that few automobile owners realize how much it actually costs to run a car. In a report issued in 1967, the AAA found that the cost of actually operating the average car, including such items as gas, oil, thousand-mile checkups, and other maintenance expenses, runs to about $380 per year, or 3.8 cents per mile. (The average car is a middle-priced model driven ten thousand miles a year.) Of course, the fixed costs of owning a car are even higher. These are the costs you have even if you never take your car from your driveway. Whether you drive it or not, it loses value month by month. Even a car that has never been driven may be worth only half its original value after two or three years. When this depreciation in the value of a car is added to the cost of insurance and registration, the AAA says the total figure is 13.6 cents per mile, or $1,360 per year, for a car driven ten thousand miles annually. A Cadillac will cost more than this; a Volkswagen will cost much less.

Many people are shocked to discover that the costs of running an automobile are so high, yet it is essential for good money management to keep these figures in mind. It is too easy to drive a car ten or fifteen miles to take advantage of a "bargain" that saves you a quarter when you are not aware that it will cost you three or four times more than the amount to be saved to get to the store and back.

Also included under this heading should be the average monthly cost of other means of travel—bus, taxi, public transportation on train, subway, or other means to get to and from work, etc.

Expenses of this kind may be cut to some extent in an emergency, although you probably cannot eliminate them entirely.

For example, if you live outside the central part of a major city, you might find it an extreme hardship to live without an automobile; a car may be necessary, not only for getting to and from work, but also for shopping. However, cutting down on the use of your car is a different matter. The average car owner can save thousands of miles each year simply by avoiding unnecessary trips: planning ahead to do all his shopping in a particular area at one time; buying enough meat and groceries at the supermarket to last a week instead of making several trips a week; and so on. If necessary, you could also cut down on beauty treatments, clothing purchases, and some food purchases.

The most easily adjustable category of spending for most people includes amounts that go for recreation, entertainment, gifts, contributions, etc. You may think you spend very little on these things, but most people, I have found, are astonished to discover how much they actually spend for personal gratification. Let me list items falling into this category:

Amounts spent each month on tobacco, liquor, wine, and beer; amounts spent on entertaining friends, such as the extra juicy prime roast beef you would not ordinarily have yourself; amounts spent on sports and hobbies—golf equipment, for example, or bingo parties, bridge luncheons, and ball games; amounts spent on cultural advancement—books, magazines, concerts, records, and membership dues and other expenses for any societies you belong to; amounts spent on vacations—not only your annual vacation but also weekends you spend away from home; amounts spent on food eaten out, including not only restaurant meals but also snacks at the soda fountain or candy counter; and amounts spent on pets.

Your most easily adjustable expenses may also include gifts and contributions to various causes: amounts you spend at Christmas and on birthdays for relatives and friends; flowers for sick friends; and contributions to church and other charities, as well as what you may give someone standing on a street corner with his hand outstretched.

"Why is it necessary to keep detailed records of my spending? I have a good idea of where my money goes."

Excuse me, but I doubt it. I have made many tests over the years, asking men and women first to estimate offhand how much they spend on their easily adjustable expenses and then to list, item by item, how much they really do spend. Almost without exception, they discover that they spend much more on these items than they realize. Those who spend the most in these ways often finally admit that money seems to dribble through their hands.

Yet you must know what is happening to your money before you can decide intelligently whether you like what is happening. No one would deny that it is pleasant to go out for a morning coffee break, to enjoy a restaurant meal, or to attend a theater without feeling guilty about it or fearing that you are wrecking your budget for the month. Nevertheless, before you can really enjoy that impulsive cocktail, you have to know that it will not cause you any serious financial hardship.

"Are you suggesting that we keep a budget?"

No, I am not proposing a budget for you. A budget is a plan of spending you hope to follow. What I suggest is a more factual proposition: an account of what you actually spend your money for. I can virtually guarantee that if you have not made such a list recently, you will encounter some surprises.

A woman with four children told me that she had cut her expenses to the bare bones and that there was no possible way to cut further. She was very much overweight, so I assumed that perhaps she was spending more on food and snacks than she realized. "We believe in living well," she said. "Maybe we spend a *little* too much on food, but not enough to make a difference."

Nevertheless, she agreed to record her expenses for a month. It was easy to see where her money went. What she spent on snacks alone was enough to make the difference between financial solvency and insolvency. Every night she and her husband and children watched television with potato chips, cookies, peanuts, soft drinks, or beer by their sides. At the end of one month, this woman discovered that her family's habits of eating and drinking between meals cost $68.00—slightly more than $2.00 every day. Whenever she and her husband went shopping, they habitually stopped for such things as hamburgers, coffee, and cake. Actually, this item of snacks alone made the difference between living on their income and not living on it. The point is that she had no idea how much she was spending on those things until she made a careful tabulation for one month.

I wish I could say that she used this information, eliminated snacks, lost thirty pounds herself while her family slimmed down as well, and that they are now all trim and healthy and living comfortably within their income. The fact is that in making her analysis of her monthly spending, she discovered that a large amount was going out to pay off a fifteen-year mortgage and that she could reduce her housing payments by extending her mortgage for a twenty-five-year period. Although she thought she could now spend her money on snacks without feeling guilty, she was actually spending a great deal more on interest on the borrowed money.

I suggest that you go to your local variety or stationery store and buy a little account book to record your daily expenditures for the various items I have discussed above. Keep this record as conscientiously as you can for at least one month, and preferably three months. With this record in hand, you can determine how much of your income goes toward the things you really want it to go for and how much is dribbled away on trivialities. You may not find yourself "wasting money." On the contrary, you may find you are spending entirely too much on things of supposedly lasting value. Some people go overboard on insurance, for example, and even on education. One mother sends her child to a private school and a private summer camp, yet she denies him simple toys and other pleasures.

Keeping a record of your actual expenditures will reveal

countless ways in which you can cut your expenses if you are so inclined. One couple had two cars—both large, high-powered vehicles in the $5,000 price range when new. They knew the cars were costly to maintain, but they did not realize how costly, partly because the husband bought gas and oil for the car he drove, the wife paid cash for her gas and oil, and occasionally they used credit cards for such purchases. Only when they tabulated all the expenses did they realize that the use of two large, gas-hungry cars with heavy insurance rates was running more than $200, on the average, per month. They sold both cars and bought compact models instead—a move designed to cut their expense almost in half. Their savings, incidentally, removed a sore spot between them, because the wife had complained for several years that they were always "too broke" to visit her relatives two thousand miles away.

Another woman had the habit of dropping off her dresses at a dry cleaning establishment on her way to work and picking them up on her way back. Until she began to keep records, she did not realize that it cost her almost $30.00 a month for this service. Now she waits until Saturday and takes her garments to a do-it-yourself dry cleaning place, where she can get a machine-load done for $2.00. Thus she now has about $20.00 a month to use for other purposes.

People often underestimate the amounts spent on liquor, particularly in cocktail lounges and restaurants. One man often stopped off at a cocktail lounge for a few drinks before going home to dinner. He knew how much the drinks were costing, of course, but he failed to consider that he invariably left the bartender a tip or that he often felt in such an expansive mood after the drinks that he took a taxi home instead of a bus. Actually this habit was costing him twice as much as he realized.

"What do I do after compiling my record of expenses showing how my money is being used?"

Your next step should be further questioning: Do I like what

I see? Does this record indicate that I am moving toward the goals I have set for myself? Or does it reveal serious gaps in my financial progress?

In general, those whose expenses exceed their incomes, and who are not putting aside certain amounts for future use, are dissatisfied with how things are going. In spite of what one reads about this "irresponsible" generation, I find that most people want the security of building financial resources for the future—sufficient money to house and educate their children, to provide for their old age, and to leave something to give their children a good start in life. Of course, some give no thought for tomorrow, figuring that the government will take care of them if necessary. Nevertheless, most people—particularly those interested enough to seek my advice—want to keep their expenditures below their income so that a certain amount every month can go into savings or investments, to provide comfort and security for them in their later years.

Of course, the way you want to spend your money is different in at least some ways from that of anyone else. Perhaps you get great satisfaction out of owning two big cars and would die of embarrassment if anyone saw you in a tiny imported one. Perhaps an hour spent in a cocktail lounge before dinner is the big event of your day, and you get no equivalent satisfaction by having drinks at home. Perhaps you are perfectly satisfied with how you are handling your income, and your record of expenditures confirms your opinion that you are exactly on target. Even under such circumstances, your record-keeping serves a useful purpose, for it reassures you that you are on the right track. More likely, you will find that you are spending more on certain items than you think you should and that by being more alert you could get the same goods and services you are now getting, at a lower cost.

I can certainly help you, in the pages that follow, to increase your purchasing power through smarter shopping practices and wiser use of credit, but in the matter of bringing your spending in line with your income, I can merely serve as a cheerleader. In the final analysis, it is up to you—to your power to say "no" to the impulse to gratify your desires of the moment. What separates the adults from the children is not just knowing what to do but having the willpower to do it. I could take two persons, instruct them in money management, and give them a test at the end of the course. The two might well score the same marks, indicating that both know equally well what *should* be done. One will then go out and do it. The other will not. It is up to you to decide which kind of person you want to be.

THREE **Are You Really a Smart Shopper?**

"I probably spend as much time as anyone searching for bargains, going to sales, and so on. I consider myself a smart shopper, but my husband accuses me of 'spending a dollar to save a cent.' How would you describe a smart shopper?"

Of all the people I have advised about their financial affairs down through the years, few ever freely admitted that they were not wise when it came to shopping. A woman will admit to doing foolish things occasionally—buying things that she does not need or that are overpriced—but in her mind these are exceptions. The average man will also fight to the death any suggestion that, aside from a few foolish moments now and then, he does not know how to get maximum value for his money.

The reality, however, may be an entirely different matter. For example, one woman drives fifteen miles to a "discount" food supermarket, where prices on every item are a few cents less than in a market close to her home. "On a $20.00 grocery order, I always save at least a dollar," she told me proudly.

"But what about the gas and oil you use? And how about the value of your time—the hour or so you spend to get to and from this supermarket, plus the extra time you spend in line at the check-out counters because the place is jammed with bargain-seekers?"

"Oh, I don't worry about that. My husband buys the gas, and I wouldn't be spending my time doing anything else anyway."

From a strictly business point of view, this woman spends more for her bargains than she saves. Yet she will fight the idea that she is not a smart shopper. Since she is doing what she wants and feels satisfied with her shopping methods, I cannot argue with her too strongly. Yet if she complains to me that she lacks sufficient income to buy all the things she thinks she should have, that is another story.

Oscar Wilde coined a comment every woman who wants to consider herself a smart shopper should take to heart. Wilde said of one character that he knew "the price of everything and the value of nothing." In order to determine whether any goods and services are worth what you are asked to pay, you must consider not only the price of the item itself but many other factors that add up to the value that item has for you.

For instance, the woman who shops at the supermarket fifteen miles away looks only at what she pays at the check-out counter and no further. She does not consider the cost of running her car, yet it can easily be proved that she would do better by patronizing the higher-priced store nearer home.

"What factors should a smart shopper always take into consideration?"

The price of the item as compared to that of other items. One girl went to a store having an end-of-season "close-out sale" of winter dresses in March. She bought a $30.00 garment for $15.00, and it seemed to be a wonderful bargain. She put the dress in her closet, planning to begin wearing it in September. Another girl waited for the new styles in August and paid the full list price. Which one was smarter? In this case, the girl who bought the latest model wore it all season and felt in style all the while. The girl who bought the bargain merchandise wore it a few times and then became dissatisfied because it was not up to date. It cost her about $2.00 each time she wore her dress, whereas each time the second girl wore her dress it cost her only about 30 cents.

Buying "end-of-season" bargains is often a good way of saving money, but it is not as foolproof as you might imagine. It probably works best on items that do not go out of style quickly or that you will not want to sell later. For example, you may find a real bargain in a television set, dishwasher, or refrigerator at the end of a model year, because you probably do not intend to trade in the item for a newer model later on but will use it until it wears out and then discard it. On the other hand, end-of-season buys on automobiles may be less advantageous than you think. The reason is that existing cars automatically lose value whenever a new model comes out. If you get a $400 discount on a $2,300 automobile in August, you will discover in September that your car is worth much less than you paid for it for the simple reason that it has depreciated automatically.

The use you intend to make of the item. A girl had to wear very high heels for her junior college graduation ceremony. It was unlikely that she would wear such shoes again. She wanted to buy them at the most expensive store in town, where the price was $30.00. Another store sold shoes for $5.99. Of course, these were made of the thinnest leather and would probably lose their shape after a few wearings. The girl's mother insisted upon buying the cheaper shoes, and I think her judgment was correct. The cheap shoes would serve the purpose intended. On the other hand, it might be penny-wise and pound-foolish to buy cheap shoes for day-in, day-out use. Not only will more expensive shoes usually last longer, they will retain their shape better and provide better support for your arches.

If you consider how you will be using the items involved, you can probably save a great deal on linens, sheets, towels, pillowcases, and the like. In most big cities, some stores regularly carry imperfects or seconds in such items. Sometimes the imperfections are so slight that one must look extremely hard to find them. They are, in fact, the kind of imperfections that might develop after the article has been used only once or twice. Yet the price of such imperfects may be as much as

50 per cent less than the cost of a "perfect" equivalent item.

On the same basis, it will pay you to stock up on staple items when they are on sale. You know that you will be using soap and soup, toothpaste, and similar items. Buy them in quantity at sale prices.

When you consider items in the light of the use to be made of them, you may find yourself patronizing "thrift shops," clothing exchanges, or other stores that specialize in used clothing. Such stores are a particularly important source of savings for parents of small children; they know that youngsters quickly outgrow their clothing and that expensive articles will have to be replaced in months—perhaps weeks. In many places, women's clubs, church organizations, and parent-teacher groups operate clothing exchanges where one may sell or contribute items of clothing. The outlet then resells them, often at ridiculously low prices, using the profits to finance some of its programs. These shops help everybody: the owner of the outgrown clothing gets some money for them and recovers part of their original cost; the exchange gets income to carry on its other work; the customer gets usable merchandise at only a small fraction of what it would cost new.

How you will use what you buy is an important factor to consider when shopping for food. Many foods cost more because of their appearance, not because they taste better or are more nutritious. This is true, for instance, of canned tomatoes. Lower-grade tomatoes may be just as flavorsome as the Grade A type costing as much as 10 cents more per large can. If you intend to use the tomatoes for cooking, where appearance does not count—in making spaghetti sauce, for instance—one grade serves as well as the other. Grade B eggs are inferior to Grade A eggs for boiling or poaching, but they are just as serviceable for baking. When recipes call for milk, you can use the dry, powdered kind at half the cost of liquid whole milk.

You can cut meat costs substantially by considering how the meat will be prepared and served. There are six official grades of beef: *prime*, top-quality grade with lots of fat, juicy and tender; *choice*, just a little less juicy; *good*, which tends to be leaner; *standard*, which has little fat; *commercial*, which is generally cut from older cattle; and *utility*, which comes from the very oldest cattle.

If you intend to broil steak, prime beef will undoubtedly be best; it is easy to cut and chew, the kind that melts in your mouth. A broiled steak of utility grade will be tough and stringy, difficult to cut, and lacking both tenderness and juiciness. But if you plan to use the meat for pot roasting, stewing, boiling, or ground up as hamburgers, the lowest grade may suit your purposes as well as prime. A stew made of low-priced meat cooked for a long time under slow, moist heat often tastes as good as top-grade meat cooked the same way. In fact, the real test of a good cook is not how well he prepares a prime quality steak but how well he turns economical grades of meat into tasty stews and casseroles.

Often you can get excellent buys in fruits and vegetables with blemishes that do not affect their quality. For example, clean, crack-free potatoes generally bring more at the market than dirty ones or those that show little cracks or other blemishes. Yet the latter taste just as good when cooked. Blotched apples, cabbage with yellowed outer leaves, and mottled bananas may well taste better than the prettier kinds, for producers have tended in recent years to favor crops that keep their appearance well even if they suffer in flavor as a result.

On the other hand, decayed fruit and vegetables, marked down in price, may be the most expensive in the long run if you have to throw away the greater part of them. This makes the cost per edible unit higher.

Convenience of shopping. A man recently needed a bale of peat moss to use as mulch for the plants and shrubs in his garden. He had to choose between driving two miles to a discount store where the bale sold for $4.25 or asking a nearby hardware store to deliver one at a cost of $6.00. He chose the latter course.

Was his decision to pay almost 50 per cent more a wise one?

Offhand, one might say no. When one considers all the circumstances, however, a different picture emerges.

The man went to business during the week and could work in his garden only on Saturdays. He considered gardening recreation—something he could not say for the routine of going to the discount house, waiting in line, carrying the bale to the car himself, then removing the bale from the car and tugging it to where he wanted to work. Going to the discount store, he reasoned, would cost him an hour's time as well as inconvenience. The extra $1.75 he spent at the local store seemed well worthwhile. Another person, who had the time to spare and could combine his purchase of the peat moss with other items he needed, might consider buying from the local merchant sheer extravagance.

Employed persons, in particular, could be more considerate of the value of their own time when determining where to make their purchases. An example of this was given me by a young bargain-conscious couple needing a new refrigerator and clothes washer and dryer for a home they had just bought. The girl decided to lose a day's pay—$20.00—in order to accompany her husband to different appliance stores. They already knew what brands they wanted, so the only problem was to find the store with the lowest prices. After visiting six stores, they bought $800 worth of appliances for $620. "We saved $180 on the deal," she said triumphantly, "so it made good sense to give up a day's wages of $20.00."

On the surface, her reasoning seemed sound. However, I asked her how much they would have had to pay at the first discount store they went to—the one where they normally would have bought the equipment. This store's price was $628, so that actually, by going to five other stores and spending money to get to and from them, they saved only $8.00 more than they could have saved by buying their appliances at the first shop in half an hour's time, even during their lunch hour. By taking the day off, therefore, the wife had a net loss of $12.00. To this day, however, she thinks that by taking the day off she saved $160.

Obviously, a successful executive's time is worth more than a grocery clerk's. Why should you use your high-priced time to pick groceries off a shelf when someone earning only one-quarter as much per hour could do the job? On the other hand, someone with low earnings per hour might save a great deal simply by investing time in a search for bargains.

"Is there any easy way to distinguish a good shopper from a poor one?"

Most people who have trouble managing their money the way they'd like to lack self-discipline when shopping. I am almost tempted to say that all bad money managers act impulsively. They go to a store intending to buy a certain item and somehow leave with more things than they had planned to get. Or they plan to buy one item at a certain price, and they leave paying a much higher price. Or they go to a store just intending to "look around" and emerge with something they had not planned to get and, worse, do not really need.

A typical example of impulse buying is the story of a couple who found their future mortgaged for several years simply because of one hasty act by the husband. This couple had a late-model compact car. They decided that they needed a second car, one that would enable the husband to drive to work without leaving his wife without transportation all day long. This car, they agreed, was to be bought secondhand and was to be a tiny foreign model that would give thirty miles to a gallon of regular gas and require almost no maintenance. The husband went to an auto dealer who sold both used and new cars and asked to see one fitting this description. The salesman had none of that type to sell, so he proceeded to try to sell a new car. He pointed out that a new car would come with a two-year guarantee and would have a high resale value. Most of all, it would have modern conveniences—power brakes, power steering, various safety features. The customer was swept off his feet, not only by the glamorous appeal of the new car, but by the fact that he could get it by laying out little more cash than he would need to swing a used car. So he signed a contract for a new car, committing himself to paying out over a three-year period $1,800 more than he had intended—$600 a year, $50.00 a month, or $12.00 a week. When he got home and told his wife what he had done, it was too late for her to reason him out of it.

Another couple whose income and outgo habits I analyzed went impulsively overboard several times each year—enough to keep them in financial hot water. Typically, they once went to a repair shop to have their black and white portable television set repaired. The mechanic-dealer told them that he would have to charge $35.00 for his work, but that the set was not worth it. He offered $50.00 for the old box as a trade-in against a $480 color television set. They succumbed, and in one moment their spending power was thrown out of whack for months. Another year, they saved $650 to pay for a two-week vacation. When they went to buy the airline tickets for their trip, they were told how easy it was to get transportation on credit. Instead of $350 in cash for hotels and meals, they now had $600. They spent it all, and when they returned home, they were $250 in debt—not at all what they had planned.

Many impulse spenders make up in persistence what they lack in dramatics. They do not spend on big things, but their money just dribbles away anyway. It is a fact that when a woman shops alone at a grocery supermarket, she sticks mainly to buying items she needs. As soon as someone else goes with her, however, the impulse to buy special things becomes stronger. The children see cake, cookies, and other good things and put them in the shopping basket. When her husband goes with her, he may spend a great deal of time in the delicatessen department, putting pickles, sliced meats, potato chips, and other snack items in the cart. Studies have shown that the more people in the shopping party, the higher the amount rung up at the cash register. Of course, occasional snacks should not wreck the average budget, but a grocery bill habitually a few dollars higher than it might be adds up to a substantial sum in a year's time.

It takes a great deal of self-control and determination to avoid impulse buying. It may be impossible to eradicate entirely, and I doubt whether anyone would want to do so anyway. There is a certain satisfaction in being able to buy an unplanned-for cup of coffee and doughnut or an unbudgeted ice cream soda at a snack bar, in picking up a new hair cream or other product you have heard about on television and would like to try, and so on. Life would be much duller if we could never give in to any desires unless we planned them fully in advance. But those who get into money troubles do not generally confine themselves to satisfying an occasional inexpensive whim. They do it habitually—and often with substantial sums.

The reason it takes conscious determination to resist your impulses to buy what you don't need is that billions of dollars are spent every year on advertising designed to get you to do the opposite. Much advertising is created to make you want to buy immediately. Many millions of dollars are spent every year, for example, to make packages so appealing that you cannot resist buying them. In this "age of obsolescence," consumers are often urged to buy new products, not because the old ones no longer work well, but just because they are old.

To a large extent, the whole credit card system is a force working toward impulse buying. One woman, to avoid buying things she did not need, never went shopping unless she left most of her money at home. Then she made the mistake of getting a credit card enabling her to charge anything and everything. The first month, her credit purchases put her in debt by several hundred dollars. She turned in the credit card and went back to her old way of doing things.

Even if you never get a credit card, you can find stores all over town willing to give you credit on a "thirty-day basis." To resist "easy credit," you have to steel yourself with the notion that credit is never cheap; while a loan may be easy to get, it is much harder to repay. And you have to remember this most of all when a persuasive salesman is dangling a most attractive item in front of you and telling you how easily you can walk out of the store with it. (I tell you what you should know about credit in the next chapter.)

When you are tempted to buy on impulse, you would also do well to remember that few if any opportunities arise but once in a lifetime. The product that seems so irresistible in the store today is likely to be there tomorrow as well. You will lose nothing by spending a night thinking over any major purchases you are tempted to make, calmly determining the cost of the item itself and of the credit involved, and considering what this major purchase would do to your overall budget and what things you would have to do without in order to have it. Maybe after calm and careful consideration you will still want to make the purchase. If so, you will be doing it with reason, lessening the danger that you will later regret your actions.

"Someone came to my door and offered me a lifetime painting job for the outside of my home for no more than a regular job would cost. I turned him down flat. Now I wonder, did I do the right thing?"

Your financial plans can be thrown out of kilter for months, and possibly years, if you succumb to just one or two of the various kinds of gyps and rackets now prevalent. Homeowners in particular have been prey to such rackets for many years. Individuals representing themselves as government inspectors call at the door offering to inspect a furnace or test the plumbing system. Before the homeowner realizes what is happening, the "inspector" finds many things seriously wrong and paints a grim picture of what will happen to the family's health or safety unless the situation is remedied at once. Often, the homeowner becomes terrified by the story and, concerned for his family's welfare, signs a contract obligating the family to pay hundreds and perhaps even thousands of dollars for work that may be completely unnecessary. Homeowners should beware of any such offer with a twenty-year or "lifetime" guarantee. They should also avoid doing business with any contractors who are not established locally.

Another form of racket you must protect yourself against is known as bait advertising. This unethical practice is advertising that offers for sale merchandise the advertisers have no intention of selling. For instance, some stores are said to have television sets "nailed to the floor." They advertise these sets at ridiculously low prices. Try to buy one, and the salesman will do everything in his power to stop you. If nccessary, hc will tell you that the advertised sets are no good, that all of them have been sold, that you will have to wait months for delivery, or anything else he can think of. His intention, of course, is to sell you something more expensive. If you are "baited" this way, leave the store and complain to the Better Business Bureau.

To avoid being gypped, you must know when a bargain is really a bargain. You must be able to recognize quality—to know whether goods or services will give the performance you expect. You must know comparative prices. You must be realistic enough to know that nobody gives you something for nothing or next to nothing. Above all, you must know the condition of your own pocketbook, for nothing is a bargain if you can't afford it, don't need it, or can't use it.

FOUR **Using Credit Successfully**

"Almost every time I pick up a newspaper or magazine, I read something about the gap between the generations. The old standards former generations were brought up on seem to have gone by the boards. Take the way young people view the matter of credit, borrowing money for the things they want even when they have no plans to pay for them; don't you think this kind of buying has gotten out of hand?"

I certainly do. I get many questions like this, usually from older people who think that owing money to anyone is the greatest of crimes—a sign of weakness and degradation, something they would not want people to know they did any more than they would want it known that they had leprosy. On the other hand, I know young married couples who never pay cash for anything except their day-to-day living expenses. They obtain their cars, furniture, vacations, and wardrobes all on a basis of so much down and so much per month. Paying cash for such items is as unthinkable to them as buying anything on credit is to people who have been trained differently.

I find myself in the middle on this question. I believe that the intelligent use of credit can be a tremendous help in attaining one's lifetime goals. On the other hand, I think that using credit for anything and everything is a shortsighted habit that can lead to financial ruin.

"How can I tell how much it will cost me to use credit?"

This is the most important question about credit. Only if you know how much more a store that lets you use a monthly account charges you than a store that sells only for cash, or how much interest you must pay when buying on the installment plan, will you be able to decide intelligently whether to pay now or later. Make no mistake about this: when you buy on credit, either charging your purchases and being billed later or paying so much down and the rest in installments, you are going to have to pay more, directly or indirectly.

The minute a store begins selling on credit, it increases its overhead. It may have to borrow money to pay for the merchandise it lets you have on credit, and it must pay interest on such money. It has to consult—for a fee—a credit bureau that investigates each prospective credit-user's ability to pay. It must hire employees to keep its charge-account books, to send out bills, and to make sure that payments are made in time. It must hire legal help to collect its bad debts. And because some of its charge customers will not pay their bills and it will be unable to collect from them for one reason or other, it must make more of a profit on the goods for which it can collect. All of these factors mean that a store *must* charge more to cover the extra expenses a credit operation involves.

Many young people who have never lived in a period when it was considered wrong and maybe even sinful to owe money take credit so for granted that they do not realize how much extra its use can cost them. A furniture salesman told me in amazement, "Young couples shopping to furnish their homes often never even ask me the price of the living room suites and bedroom sets they want. All they think about is how much they will have to pay per month. When we try to tell them how much the interest will cost them, they give an impatient yawn."

Some couples, on the other hand, are very price-conscious. They go from store to store, comparing tags on the items they want to buy. When they find the store with the lowest price, they consider their shopping finished. They then sign a contract to pay the price in monthly installments, disregarding the fact that they may have to pay interest charges much greater than if they had bought at the first store and used the best possible credit arrangements. It is often the case that if you buy something costing a few hundred dollars or more on credit, your biggest savings can be made not by seeking out the store carrying the item at the lowest price (although you can save this way too), but by shopping for the lowest-cost credit you can get. The reason is that credit charges on a $500 item, paid out over a twenty-four-month period, may cost you as much in interest as $75.00 or more, or as little as $20.00—a spread of $55.00.

"When (if ever) is it wise to use credit?"

I would list five circumstances:

1. When it allows you to have something you really need or would suffer without. A woman whose doctor diagnosed her condition as appendicitis and told her she needed an operation immediately did not have enough savings to pay the surgeon's fee and the hospital charges, but after she had the operation, she took out a personal loan to pay the bills. She would have been foolish—to say the least—to stick to her principles and not have the operation until she had the cash in hand.

Another couple with small children lived in a suburb and had one car. The husband commuted to work by train, and the wife used the car during the day for shopping, to take her youngsters to doctors and dentists, to drive them to and from school when it rained, and for other errands. The husband was offered a better job, at a place that could be reached only by car. The couple decided that they needed a second car and took an installment loan to pay for it: a sound decision.

A young mother's washing machine suddenly stopped functioning, and the repairman said it was not worth fixing. Because she had to wash diapers and other clothing every day, she needed another machine immediately. To wait until she had the cash would have been folly. She had a new machine delivered that same day, signing a contract to pay for it in monthly installments.

In these examples, credit served a worthwhile purpose. It made available immediately goods or services without which the persons' security might have been endangered. The sacrifice involved in waiting until they could have paid cash would have been too great, when measured against the extra amount they had to pay for the convenience of using credit. Of course, it would have been better in the instances I cited above if the parties involved had had savings and were able simply to write a check for what they had needed.

2. When you can derive lasting, long-term benefit from your purchase—for example, when buying a house. Years ago, some people considered it evidence of moral weakness for a family to mortgage their home. A husband and wife were supposed to save for years on end until they could pay the purchase price of their home in full. If they had a mortgage from a banker (in the former popular image, one with a glass eye), they were in danger of being thrown out of their house if the wage earner became temporarily unable to meet his payments in time.

Today, it is advisable for a home-buyer to pay as little of the total price as possible (perhaps only 5 per cent) when he moves in and to pay the remainder in monthly installments over as many as thirty years. We applaud this practice, because it enables a young couple to enjoy the advantages of their own home when they need it most—when their family is growing up—and also to pay it off in dollars made cheaper by inflation.

Education is another item usually worth going into debt for. Generally, the period of life during which one can attend school, college, or a university is quite limited. If an individual does not complete his education in his twenties, the likelihood that he will do so later is markedly decreased. Hence, it would be foolish for him to quit college because he does not want to borrow money to pay the tuition.

Furthermore, a strong case can be made for the idea that

borrowing money for education is a sound financial investment. Each thousand dollars spent on college tuition, for example, will be worth at least twenty times as much in the increased earning power it gives the person with a degree or degrees over his working lifetime. In fact, none of the other usual investments—in real estate, stocks, or bonds, for example—provide as great a return as the dollar invested in education. And I am not even considering the personal satisfaction, sense of fulfillment, prestige, and enlarged horizons the educated person receives.

3. When the convenience of using credit offsets its added costs. An example is the electrical service that comes into your home. It would be a great inconvenience if you had to put a quarter or a half-dollar in a vending machine in order to keep the current flowing. If you ran out of change at a critical moment, your whole living routine would be disrupted. Utility companies' practice of providing this service and billing you later is perfect evidence that credit can sometimes be a great convenience.

A business woman I know has a charge account at a small grocery store of the old-fashioned "Mom and Pop" type. Every item she buys probably costs her 15 or 20 per cent more than it would at a supermarket down the street. But she phones this store from her office, orders the groceries she needs, and when she arrives at her apartment door, the bag of groceries has already been delivered. She believes that the convenience and the saving in time outweigh the credit cost.

It may even be worthwhile to use credit to take advantage of sales. Many stores run regular year-end and inventory sales on appliances, home furnishings, clothing, and other costly items. Contractors often offer lower prices during their off seasons—a furnace installer does jobs in July and August for 25 per cent less than he charges in December. Even including the credit charges, the total cost of buying items on sale may be less than it would be if you paid the regular price in cash.

4. When "charging it" will provide you with records that help reduce your taxes. The amount of this savings depends

upon your tax bracket. Be sure to find out what tax bracket you are in. Many persons with out-of-pocket expenses connected with their businesses have found that tax collectors can be extremely finicky about demanding specific proof—receipts, itemized records, canceled checks—before allowing deductions. The increased use of credit cards by businessmen to substantiate the costs of entertaining at restaurants, for example, is directly related to the need for adequate records. Although it is evident that businesses extending such credit raise their prices to cover the additional cost, the customers reason that the savings in taxes made possible by having itemized receipts more than offset this extra expense.

5. When buying on credit is the most effective way of saving. To my way of thinking this is a weak reason, but for many people it is the strongest incentive for saving. They reason that when they are forced to make monthly payments (on an automobile, a television set, etc.) they are required to put aside a certain sum every month. They make these payments out of their regular income and do not dip into savings for them. They argue that if they withdrew the money from their savings accounts and paid cash, they would not "repay" themselves with a certain amount every month as easily as they would pay someone else. In effect, they pay the price of installment buying because they feel that it enables them to save amounts they would otherwise take from their savings account. They use installment buying to substitute for their own lack of willpower.

"What would you exclude from your list of things it is desirable to buy on credit?"

Obviously, I consider it unwise to go into debt for items you do not really need, items that satisfy your desire of the moment but will be only a memory when the bill arrives—and when the advantages of using credit do not more than offset its cost. On this list I would include expensive vacations, nondeductible restaurant meals, and luxury items not necessary for health or welfare. Your opinion about what is "necessary" may differ from mine, of course, but I am convinced that the average person can do without many more things than he usually realizes. He wants to start where his parents left off.

"There are some things we absolutely must *buy on credit. How can we shop for the most economical credit terms?"*

A typical person today expects to go into debt at least a few times in his life. Even if he has been brought up in the tradition of never buying anything until he has the cash in hand, there will be occasions when he will want to borrow something—to buy a home or a car, to pay for unexpected medical expenses, to finance the education of his children, and perhaps for lesser purposes. It is important to remember that whenever you borrow, the conditions under which you borrow will usually be the most important factor to consider. For instance, you may be able to buy a house for $1,000 less than the price for an identical house, but if you fail to get advantageous mortgage terms, you may wind up paying considerably more, in the form of higher interest rates over a period of time. Just as you can buy a dress or suit of clothes at one store for 20 to 30 per cent less than the identical garment costs at another place, so too it is possible to pay less for credit by borrowing from one lender instead of another. Often what you save by getting the least expensive credit may be greater than the actual savings on the ticket price of the merchandise.

A second point to remember is that there are different kinds of credit. For the purpose of simplification, let me separate them into two categories: long-term and short-term. Long-term credit I would consider as anything running three years or more. A home mortgage fits into this category. Short-term credit must be paid within three years, and usually much sooner. It might be a charge account at a department store, whereby you do not have interest charges if you pay your bills within thirty or sixty days but have to pay at rates running up to 1½ per cent per month after that. The short-term category might include a loan on a new automobile requiring you to pay its cost in monthly installments over a twenty-four- or thirty-month period. Generally—and except when there is a thirty- or sixty-day "grace" period—the shorter the loan, the higher the interest rate.

Let us consider the major types of credit, terms of payment, interest rates, and other provisions. These include:

A regular charge account at a store. Almost every place at which you buy (even drugstores, gas stations, and variety stores, once known as "five and tens") will gladly open an account for you. You can shop quickly and buy what you want without having to carry large amounts of cash with you. When the bill arrives, you pay it within thirty days or so. It seems so easy. But if for some reason you fail to pay within the specified period, steep interest charges—often amounting to 1½ per cent of the unpaid balance—accumulate. People accustomed to thinking of annual interest rates in terms of 5 and 6 per cent may consider 1½ per cent a low figure. But note: this 1½ per cent is the interest charge per *month*, not per year. Let us say that you buy $200 worth of goods on a store charge account, fully intending to pay the bill when it arrives. But something else comes up (as it has a habit of doing), and when the bill arrives, you don't have the cash to pay it. That 1½ per cent charge amounts to $3.00 *per month*—a sum you might drive many miles out of your way or spend an hour or two at a bargain counter to save. If you do not pay your debt after another thirty days, you also owe interest on the accumulated interest, or another 3.5 cents. If you are unlucky enough to have to let your bill run six months, you will have to pay almost $20.00 more than the purchase price in order to get out from under. If you had to pay that $20.00 extra for your purchases in the first place, you might never have made them.

The point is that such charge accounts are a convenient way of shopping for people who are reasonably sure that they can pay the bills upon receipt without incurring "service charges." They are also satisfactory for those hardheaded enough to realize that they will ultimately have to pay for what they buy.

Continuing credit plan. Many banks issue credit cards that enable the holders to buy at a large number of shops, restaurants, hotels, etc., in the community. Bills from these places are sent to a central clearinghouse and charged against your account. When you begin the plan, the bank may specify a certain maximum amount it will permit you to buy on credit. This amount may be as much as $5,000. Each month, you are billed for credit purchases you have made, and a service charge—perhaps 1½ per cent of the "unpaid balance"—is tacked on. Amounts unpaid at the end of thirty days have another interest charge tacked on against them.

The advantage, if you want to call it that, of such plans is that you can buy in many different stores and buy almost everything you want on one credit card. But the fact that this is so easy to do is what makes it so dangerous. The actual cost of this credit, like that of store charge accounts, may run up to more than 20 per cent per year when the interest on the unpaid balance is included.

A hazard of this new type of charge plan is that you can easily become "hooked" and remain in debt permanently. If the experience of some who have sought my advice is any indication, many people find that their net unpaid balance keeps climbing month after month. After a few years, they reach the maximum of their credit-charging potential. Then they are committed to a permanent cost of hundreds of dollars per year on the money they owe.

Extended payment plan. This is a variation of a charge account, except that you may be given three or six months to pay without being charged interest. Some people find this type of credit very useful. One man buys most of his clothes at a semiannual clearance sale each July. Because the store knows its sales will be slack at that time, it permits customers to pay in installments in August, September, and October. If the customer does not pay on time, however, an interest charge—perhaps that gigantic 1½ per cent per month—begins to apply. One who cannot pay the charges when due risks being saddled with exorbitant interest rates.

Installment payment plan. In view of the widespread introduction of universal credit cards, the individual installment plan is becoming somewhat old-fashioned. This is the traditional kind of installment buying; for instance, you decide that you want a car costing $3,000 and then sign a contract agreeing to pay part of the price in regular monthly installments over a twenty-four-, thirty-, or thirty-six-month period. The seller usually turns your signed sales contract over to a bank or other credit agency, for a commission, and in return gets the sale price in cash at once—leaving the bank or agency with the task of collecting the monthly installments from you. Of course, they do not perform this job without charging substantial interest fees. They must protect themselves, not only against the possibility that the debt may turn out to be bad, but also to cover the commission they give the merchant and the cost of servicing your account. Sometimes they also add the cost of expensive life insurance covering the unpaid balance—their assurance that they will collect the full amount of your debt in case you die.

Such installment buying is always more expensive than the average person realizes. You can closely approximate the interest rate by a simple arithmetical calculation. First write down the total cash price of the item you are buying. Next write down the payment you will be expected to make on this purchase each month. Multiply this figure by the number of months you will have to make it. This will give you the total amount you will pay for the item on the installment plan. The difference between the cash price and the total of all the installments is the amount you pay for credit. When you make this calculation, you will see that on a purchase of a thousand dollars or more, the cost of using credit can run to hundreds of dollars.

To determine the interest rate in such a situation, first write down half of the cash price of the item. This is the average amount you would owe over the life of the installment contract. Next, divide the total amount you will pay in interest by the number of years the contract will run. This tells you how much interest you will pay, on average, per year. Now divide the average amount you will owe by the average amount you will pay in interest per year. *The result will be the actual interest rate you will pay on your purchase.*

For example, suppose you buy a car for $3,000. The salesman offers you an installment contract allowing you to pay $500 down and the rest over a three-year period. The balance you will owe is $2,500, and the overall average amount you will owe over the three-year period is therefore $1,250. Now let us say that your total monthly payments will be $81.03 per month. That doesn't sound like much, does it? But when you multiply that by the total number of payments—thirty-six—you will find that it amounts to $3,250 or $750 more than it would cost you if you paid cash. This calculation alone is enough to make you realize what "easy credit" can cost.

Let's carry the calculation further. The average amount you will pay out in interest each year is $250 (one third of the $750 to be paid out over the three-year peroid). By dividing $1,250—the overall average amount owed—into $250, you get the figure 20 per cent. And that is the rate of interest you will pay to buy this car on credit under the contract the salesman is offering you.

Is this example an exaggeration? By no means. It is quite ordinary. It is possible to pay less interest when buying a car, furniture, or other "big ticket" items on the installment plan, but any plan in which the actual interest rate amounts to less than 10 per cent is a rare plan indeed.

Finance company loans. You doubtless have seen or heard advertisements for the loan companies that make these small loans. They are the "friendly" lenders who tell you that they have confidence in you even if your credit standing is no good elsewhere. To some extent, this advertising is true. You probably can borrow from a small loan company more easily than from your neighborhood bank, for example. But the fact that the loan companies are willing to make riskier loans also means that a higher percentage of their borrowers do not pay back the loan.

They have to make allowances for this higher loss ratio in the interest they charge you. Therefore, these loans are exceptionally costly.

The interest rates consumer finance companies can charge are generally fixed by the states in which they operate. These companies usually show their interest rate on a monthly basis. In a typical case, you will have to pay 2.5 per cent interest per month on the first $100 you owe, 2 per cent on the amount owed from $100 to $300, and 0.5 per cent on the rest. Thus, if you owe $500, your interest per month will amount to $7.50—or an average of 1.5 per cent. On a $300 loan, it will be 2.16 per cent. On a $100 loan, 2.5 per cent per month, which is 30 per cent per year. The lower the amount of your loan, the higher the rate of interest you have to pay.

If you take a loan from this type of company and begin making regular payments, at the end of the third or fourth month they may begin to press you or in a polite manner invite you to borrow enough more to bring the borrowed sum up to its original level. You are granted this "privilege" because you have proven yourself a good credit risk. If you succumb to this folly, you could be in debt to them for the rest of your life.

Installment bank loans. Commercial banks, which once frowned on making loans to individuals, now try to outdo each other in letting the public know their willingness to extend "instant credit." Their advertising says that you can be sure they are ready and willing to advance substantial amounts for almost any purpose, not only for serious emergencies such as a sudden hospital bill or funeral expense, but also for trivial reasons—to take a vacation because you want to "get away from it all," to buy a boat or car because you have grown tired of the old one, or just to have spending money for a week on the town. All they usually require is that you have a steady job so that if you do not make the monthly payments, they will be able to instruct your employer to deduct the amount from your salary. This procedure is known as garnishment. When an employee's wages are garnisheed, his employer is likely to consider him irresponsible and seek a convenient excuse to fire him. I mention this distasteful subject at this point because lenders sometimes give the impression that borrowers never have problems in making the payments. It is important to realize that if you fall behind in your payments by a few months, you can be reasonably certain that one day your employer will be legally required to pay part of your wages directly to the lender. There will be nothing you can do to stop this process, for in the contract you signed when you borrowed the money, you gave the lender the authority to do it.

Actually, interest rates charged by banks or installment loans run, as a rule, about twice what they seem to be. Thus, when the rate on an automobile loan is advertised at 5 per cent, it generally works out at about 10 per cent. This is because the bank figures the interest rate on the total amount you borrow, while, as I pointed out above, the average amount you owe over the life of the installment contract is only half of what it is at the beginning. So when a bank gives you a $3,000 loan, the average amount you owe over the life of the contract is $1,500. And if you must pay $150 a year for the use of that money, it works out to 10 per cent interest per year on the $1,500 you are actually borrowing. Incidentally, this 10 per cent figure is about the average of what you can expect to pay for bank installment loans at this time. In periods of very easy money, the rate may be a little less, and when money gets tight, it may rise to 12 per cent or more.

Mortgage and other collateral loans. One of the oddities of the "tight-money" situation we have recently experienced is that millions of Americans with mortgages on their homes paid lower interest rates on this borrowed money than the most strongly entrenched corporations in the country. This situation exists when mortgage loans are made during "easy money" periods for long terms—from ten to thirty years, generally—at interest rates of from 4 to 6 per cent. When these mortgages were made, of course, the individual homeowners had to agree to pay higher interest rates than the top corporations then had to pay on any money they borrowed. But in the mid-sixties, interest rates on new loans began to soar, while rates on old mortgages remained what they were when the contracts were made. In the early fifties a man took out a mortgage at 4½ per cent interest. In 1967 he inherited a large sum of money. He wanted to know whether he should pay off his mortgage, which now amounted to $8,000, or invest the same amount in bonds that paid 6 per cent. A little calculation showed that by buying the bonds and earning 6 per cent, he would make a profit of 1½ per cent, or $120 a year.

This example illustrates one of the circumstances in which it is desirable to keep your mortgage as high as possible, namely, when you can invest the money more profitably elsewhere and can get a return on it that is greater than the cost of the mortgage.

Most people could not own a home unless they obtained a mortgage loan for a substantial part of its cost. Mortgage loans generally carry lower interest rates than other types of loans available to individuals. One reason is that the mortgage lender has substantial collateral—the house itself. If the borrower fails to keep up his mortgage payments, the lender can foreclose the mortgage, take title to the house, and sell it to recover the amount he loaned. He can make his interest rates lower because he has substantial security.

This principle—lower interest rates made possible by collateral that the money lender can sell if necessary, thus reducing his risk to a minimum—explains why you also can get lower interest rates if you put up stocks, bonds, insurance policies with cash-surrender values, or savings books as security.

When you make loans against such assets as these, you are in effect drawing upon your capital—using money you have accumulated, usually over a long period of time. To repay the loan, you must either take money out of your current income or sell part of the collateral.

Collateral loans are often advisable for long-term purposes. For instance, it may be better to increase your home mortgage at low interest rates to finance your child's education than to take out a tuition loan, which may cost 12 per cent or more. Similarly, you might be better advised to increase your mortgage in order to finance lasting home improvements, such as adding attic rooms or making a basement playroom for your youngsters. On the other hand, I do not recommend cutting into your collateral savings in order to satisfy short-term impulses—taking a trip, buying a fall wardrobe, and so on.

"Whenever I borrow money, on a short- or long-term basis, I am given a large printed sheet of paper to sign. Generally it is in small print and would take me half an hour to read and understand. How important is it that I read this paper before I sign?"

Whenever you borrow from a bank, store, or other enterprise, you have to sign a contract that spells out all of the details of the loan: the conditions under which you will be expected to repay it; the amounts you will have to pay at specified times; and what rights the lender will have if you fail to make the required payments. Once you sign this document, you give the lender certain legal powers over you. This legal paper you sign is binding. If it contains provisions different from those you have been given orally, a court is likely to rule that the written contract is what counts. Make sure that you understand how much money in interest you will be required to pay and that all figures are correctly stated. All figures, such as the amount of the loan if it is a direct loan or the price of the merchandise if it is a sales contract, the amounts you will be required to pay every month, and the length of time the loan contract will run, should be on the paper before you sign it. Never leave it to the lender to fill in later.

Make sure also that you know how much extra you will have to pay if a monthly payment is delayed. Some lenders charge exorbitant amounts under these circumstances. Also make sure that the contract contains no other hidden charges. Make sure that you are aware of the rights of repossession you give the lender. In some loan contracts, for example, the lender may seize and sell just about everything you own—not just any new merchandise you buy—if you default in your payments. Also see whether you are giving him authority to seize your wages. If you are married and both you and your spouse sign a sales contract, you may be asked to give the lender the right to demand both your salaries in case of default. Also, clearly understand what you may be able to save on interest charges if you want to pay your debt in full ahead of time.

"I went to buy a new car. The salesman was very friendly until he discovered that I intended to pay cash and did not want any extras. Then you'd think I had insulted his mother or something. Friends have had similar experiences. Has cash gone out of style, and are the only good customers today those who buy on the installment plan?"

Your experience is not unusual. It seems that the least desirable customers for new cars are those with cash in hand. The reason is that in many places car salesmen work on a salary basis; they get nothing additional no matter how many cars they sell. A salesman does, however, make an additional commission if he gets a customer to buy on credit, because there is a substantial kickback from the lender who finances the car and, of course, passes the extra cost on to you. If he sells you insurance along with the finance contract, he may get as much as 20 per cent commission on the premium. Salesmen also make good commissions when they sell "extras"—power brakes, power steering, automatic transmissions, radios, heaters, and all the rest—and it is much harder to sell such extras to the buyer with cash. No wonder the salesman likes people who put down as little cash as possible.

"Hardly a week passes without my being urged to apply for some credit card or other—a card, issued by a bank, that would enable me to buy on credit at hundreds of local stores; a card that would let me charge oil, gasoline, tires, and everything else dealing with the upkeep on my automobile; charge plates good at department stores and discount houses; cards that would enable me to wine and dine at thousands of restaurants and sleep at hundreds of motels and hotels all over the world; airline credit

cards I could use to fly anywhere on earth; and so on. What do you think of the 'credit card explosion'?"

Anyone with a good income and good credit rating could probably collect a dozen or more cards entitling him to charge everything and even to borrow money. The basic question, however, is whether these cards are worth it. To answer this for yourself, you should first ask what suitable purpose any particular card would serve. For instance, would it give you a convenient record of your business expenses? Would it protect you against possible financial embarrassment—if you were out of town, would it be a convenience to have credit cards if you ran short of cash? Do long intervals elapse between the times when you receive income, so that using credit may tide you over for several weeks or so? An elderly woman who gets all of her income in the form of quarterly dividend checks sometimes runs low a few weeks before a check is due. She finds credit cards a great help to her during that interval.

Of course, if thousands of banks, stores, oil companies, and other enterprises that issue credit cards had to depend solely on those who use them for the limited purposes I outlined above, they would soon be out of business. The fact is that most firms seeking to extend credit are hoping that you will buy a great deal more, giving them a profit, not only from the sales they make, but also (when they charge interest if you fail to make your payments on time) on the money you owe them. It is no secret that many stores make more on the interest of the credit they extend than they do on the items they sell.

By making it easy for you to have what you want when you want it, the issuers of credit cards expect, of course, that you will spend much more than you would if you paid cash for everything. In this way, they encourage you to give in to your impulses and make it harder for you to keep your expenses below your income. As a typical example, a person with a credit card entitling him to eat at restaurants and pay later may be more likely to patronize more expensive places and order costlier drinks and items on the menu than he ordinarily would.

A credit card makes it easy to buy a $30.00 item instead of the $20.00 one you can really afford.

When a client recently asked me if credit cards would help him, I told him what I would tell anyone: "Having credit cards is like having a large stock of alcohol in your home. Some people can use alcohol with great discretion: they take a drink occasionally, enjoy wine with their meals, and otherwise use alcohol as an adjunct to gracious living. But if having alcohol in your home means that you will tend to drink more than you should, that it will cause physical and emotional trouble, obviously you should not keep it around. Similarly, if you can use credit cards to serve your purposes, if they are a great convenience for you, go ahead and use them. But if using them leads to trouble in any way—if you buy things on impulse you really don't need, or if you habitually pay much more for the things you buy than you would pay with cash—my advice would be to get rid of them. Get on a pay-as-you-go basis and stay there."

"Is anything being done to help the credit user become aware of the real costs of credit?"

Yes. The recently enacted Truth in Lending Bill makes it necessary for all institutions that offer credit—all banks, stores, loan companies, etc.—to inform potential customers of the true costs of the credit arrangements being considered.

FIVE Your Family and Money

"One subject on which my husband and I cannot agree and which we cannot discuss without arguments is the subject of money. Have you any idea why this is so?"

In varying forms, this is one of the questions I am asked most often. If differences over money could be resolved by married couples, the number of divorces and marital breakups would be cut dramatically.

Psychiatrists tell us that the disagreements over money that crop up between husbands and wives often have as their basic cause the question of who is going to control the marriage. Modern husbands and wives recognize that money is an all-important tool in our society. They sense—if they are not consciously aware of it—that whoever controls the purse strings usually controls the whole marriage too. So when they argue over who should spend what and for what purpose, a husband and wife may really be arguing over who should make the real decisions in the family.

When a wife buys a new living room set and commits herself and her husband to paying the cost over a period of time without consulting him, she is saying in effect that she is the one who wants to make the major decisions and that his opinions are not very important. When he leaves home alone to buy a cheap used car and returns with an expensive new model—putting the family into debt for a couple of years—he is also saying that he wants to make such major decisions all by himself. When a wife complains that her husband spends hundreds of dollars on camera equipment, sporting goods, or other hobbies while she tries to save pennies at the supermarket, she is protesting that she thinks their relationship is unfair, that he is getting more from the marriage than she is. When a wife spends a large part of the family income on beauty treatments, frequent changes of wardrobe, and the like, while her husband does not know how he will pay the monthly bills, she may be expressing her hostility to him over other circumstances in their marriage. As these examples illustrate, arguments over money may be indicative of more deep-seated disagreements. They may also indicate that the husband and wife never talked over the subject of money before marriage, as they should have.

Increased divorce rates have run side by side with the increased freedom of women and their unwillingness any longer to be silent partners as far as money is concerned. At one time, the typical husband kept his financial affairs a secret from his wife. He handled all the big bills himself, often did not consult her about his spending plans, and frequently doled out small amounts to her every day or week. His idea was that she could not be trusted to handle large sums by herself. As I have pointed out, experience has shown that women are fully as competent to handle money matters as men. In many cases they are no longer willing to sit back and say nothing about how the family income is spent. Perhaps in other cases they try to say too much, the husbands resist, and trouble ensues. In any event, if you are having trouble in your marriage over financial matters, the first question to ask is whether you and your spouse have really talked the subject over and made out a financial guide for living that is satisfactory to both of you.

If you are married and have never quarreled about money, you are a rare person indeed. Surveys show that both well-adjusted and poorly adjusted couples have difficulties in the financial area. Not long ago, researchers from the University of

Pennsylvania asked three hundred couples to list the most common cause of conflict in their marriages. Two hundred of these couples had already sought help from a marriage counselor, and the other one hundred regarded their unions as reasonably happy. All had one thing in common: they said that the major area of conflict was over the way their family income was spent and managed.

"I'm tired of listening to psychiatrists who find causes going back to the womb for everything we do. Isn't there anything couples can do by themselves to settle their money problems without going to a head-shrinker?"

Yes. Several basic, easily visible conditions generally exist when husbands and wives disagree about money. There are five general areas:

1. They have not clearly thought out or talked out the question of who is to handle the money in their family. I have seen happy marriages in which the husband pays all the important bills and decides all money problems. At the other extreme, I know husbands who are happy to give their paychecks to their wives each month, taking only a small allowance for personal needs and letting the wives pay all the bills and do all the saving, investing, and overall financial planning. In other cases, husbands and wives agree to split their income in some way. Perhaps the husband takes responsibility for the big bills—housing expenses, insurance, car payments, utilities, medical bills, and so on. Perhaps the wife has a certain amount to spend each month on food, clothing for herself and her children, and personal needs.

It seems that it is not the arrangement between husband and wife that determines whether money causes marital trouble, but rather whether both are happy about whatever arrangement they have. As Dr. Tom McGinnis points out in his book *Your First Year of Marriage*, the couples who manage money well are not necessarily those who get the most for their incomes, have the most in the bank, or seem to have the most material comforts. The modern test, he says, is not what couples do with their incomes, but whether they are happy with whatever it is they are doing. Of course the ability to take advantage of shopping opportunities, to use your money for the purposes you intend, and to have money available when you need something is a sign of technical competence. And being competent at something as important as money management can help you enjoy your marriage.

I hate to get caught in the middle of quarrels between husbands and wives over who is "right" and "wrong" in money arguments. The fact is that both may be "right" as they see it, in their own eyes. A husband whose father made the major decisions about how the family income should be spent tends to think of this as the "right way." When his wife tries to exercise more control than his mother exercised, he may decide that she is trying to run the marriage and is threatening his masculinity. On the other hand, a wife from a home in which the mother balanced the family checkbook and decided how much was to be spent on what is likely to think of this as "woman's work." If her husband gives her only a small amount every month and keeps her in the cold as far as money matters are concerned, she may feel like a second-class citizen and resent it. Who is right and who is wrong? Only the husband and wife can learn to understand why the other thinks about these questions as he or she does. Only they can try to arrive at a way of operating that takes into account how each feels. But under modern conditions of marriage, I believe that the danger of blowups will be greatly decreased if both husband and wife feel that they have a fair share of power in determining how the family income should be spent.

2. They fail to agree on basic objectives. People have all kinds of attitudes about money. One woman told me that the dollar was made to be spent as soon as she got it, because no one knew what tomorrow would bring. A man said that financial security for himself and his family was all important in his life—that he would make all kinds of sacrifices today to build up capital to provide an income if he could no longer support

his family. Obviously, if the woman holding the first point of view married the man holding the second one, they would be working at cross purposes.

It frequently happens that when a man and a woman marry, they have not really considered what their basic attitudes are. The wife then discovers with dismay that her husband is a spendthrift or miser, and the husband finds his wife running up seemingly needless bills all over town or, on the other hand, refusing to buy a decent cut of meat even for guests.

Difficulties over money often can be minimized if a prospective husband and wife talk over what they really want to do with their income—how much they want to save for the future and how much they want to spend out of their income now. In just about every case I know of in which a happily married couple has accumulated a substantial amount over the years, it almost always happens that both husband and wife are solidly agreed on what they want to do, for if one wants to save and the other wants to spend, the spender almost always can torpedo the long-range program. When the saver sees this happening, the result is some kind of conflict.

3. They disagree on methods to accomplish their goals. In one case I heard about, a serious-minded young husband and wife agreed that they would live modestly during their early years together and accumulate as much as they could in a long-range investment program. When the opportunity arose for the husband to take a second job in his spare time, he accepted eagerly. He thought that all the additional income could be saved and that his wife would therefore be pleased. Her reaction was the opposite: although she wanted to save as much as possible, she did not want to sacrifice so much of their leisure time together to do it. Clearly, there was a disagreement over methods in this case.

I have found that it is usually easier to prevent serious disagreement over methods when there is agreement on long-term objectives. In the case cited above, the husband worked at his second job for a week then quit. The experience helped the couple to the extent that they now know and agree on exactly how much of a sacrifice they are willing to make for the accumulation of savings.

4. One or the other is ignorant of the facts in the case. Recently, a middle-aged mother told me that her husband and their college-age son had had many arguments over the amount of money the young man was spending. The husband, now in his fifties, could not see how the son could spend $2.00 every day for lunch. He remembered that when he was a high school senior, during the thirties, he could buy two hot dogs and a large glass of milk for 15 cents. Now the son spent $1.00 on two hamburgers and 40 cents for a chocolate malt and still felt hungry. The father thought that his son was throwing money around; he failed to realize how much prices had gone up since he was young.

In these inflationary times, almost everybody suffers a "time lag" about prices. A husband who some years ago saw his wife buy three or four packages of groceries for $10.00 may now be shocked to discover that $20.00 will not buy as much today. A wife who remembers when she herself worked and spent 75 cents for lunch may think her husband is living luxuriously because he spends $2.00 or $3.00. Even a young couple recalling the days of 10 cent cokes and 15 cent hot dogs may find it hard to grasp the fact that these things now cost twice as much.

This failure to realize how prices have changed causes much trouble in marriages, I have found. While in most cases our own incomes have risen steadily, it shocks us to realize the extent to which prices have been rising too. The $8.00 an hour we must pay a plumber to fix a leak, the $1.00 an hour or more that baby-sitters demand, the $8.00 or $10.00 a teen-ager next door wants for shoveling snow from our driveway—all strike us as being wildly out of line. Hence the husband or wife with the responsibility of managing the family finances may find it hard to convince the other that he or she is not throwing money away when paying much higher prices than were paid only a few years ago.

5. One or the other, or both, lack the self-discipline to follow through on their objectives. Some people think that the job of financial planning is done when they have decided how they will use their incomes. They do not realize that planning is only the beginning. After agreeing on your long-term objectives, you still have the difficult problem of carrying out your plans. You must keep them foremost in mind and condition your day-by-day spending and savings patterns to conform to them.

This is where self-discipline plays a major role. As I have already pointed out, every day you will encounter pressures to spend more than your plans have allowed for. It may be anything from an extra cocktail in the restaurant to a more expensive dress or suit than you had intended to buy.

I have also cited numerous examples of how undisciplined spending can throw a financial program out of kilter for months and possibly years. It cannot be overemphasized, however, that you must constantly guard against giving in to impulses that will cause financial trouble later. I especially urge that you reread the section on impulse spending until you have it indelibly fixed in your mind that such practices can ruin you financially.

"My husband and I have two children, aged two and four. We always have trouble making ends meet. I want to take a job to bring in a second income, but my husband says that it will cost me as much to work as I can earn. Can you tell me something about this?"

At one time it was considered unthinkable for women to work, but more and more are doing it these days. As this question indicates, however, there is some uncertainty about how much a working mother can contribute to the improvement of the family's overall financial condition.

Consider these facts about women workers:

Of every hundred workers in gainful employment, 35 per cent are women. About 28,000,000 women are in the labor force—37 per cent of all women of working age. Half of these women workers are over forty years of age. Two in five are forty-five or older, and one-half of all women forty-five to fifty-four years old are in the labor force. Almost three out of five women workers are married. Of all women married and living with their husbands, 34 per cent are working. Roughly 9,500,000 mothers with children under eighteen years of age are working—3,600,000 mothers with children under six. Such working mothers are 38 per cent of all women in the labor force. About 37 per cent of all women workers work full time, all year. Another 32 per cent work part time, all year.

About 32 per cent of all employed women are clerical workers. They include 8,320,000 stenographers, typists, and secretaries. Sixteen per cent are service workers (except private-household). Fifteen per cent are operatives, chiefly in factories. Almost 14 per cent are professional and technical workers (included are 1,400,000 teachers).

In 1964—the latest year for which figures are available at this time—an average of $3,710 was received by year-round full-time women workers; $1,449 by all women with income.

Of course, I cannot advise any young mother who wants to work unless I know the details in her particular case. If she can find someone to care for her children at little or no cost, or if she has a skill that enables her to earn a better-than-average salary, it seems likely that she can come out ahead financially. On the other hand, if she cannot earn much on the outside or would have to pay a great deal to have her children taken care of while she is at work, she may end up with little or nothing extra for her efforts.

If you want to know whether it will pay you to work, you should first sit down with pencil and paper. On the left side, list how much you can earn per week. But do not think that this is the amount you will take home; you must next deduct various items. First figure federal income tax, which will come out of your salary before you even get it and which is likely to be a higher percentage of your salary than now comes out of your husband's pay. Determine from your last tax return the highest percentage of income that was deducted, inasmuch as the percentage of tax you must pay increases as your income increases.

Also deduct state and local taxes (if any) on income and also sums that are automatically taken out of your paycheck for unemployment insurance. What is left is your take-home pay—the actual amount you will add to your family income.

But it costs more for a woman to go to work than it does for one to stay close to home all day. So, on the right half of your paper, list your extra costs. First put down what you will have to pay someone each week to mind your children while you are at work. You may be fortunate in having a relative or friend who will do this free, or in having a publicly financed nursery nearby where trained people will care for them. If not, you may have to hire a maid or some kind of baby-sitter, at $1.00 an hour or more. The amount you may have to pay someone else, when measured against what you would actually take home from your job, may convince you that a full-time job does not answer your financial problem.

Other expenses are generally involved when a mother goes to work. She may have to hire someone to help with the housework—perhaps a cleaning woman once or twice a week. She may have to pay extra for laundry because she now sends it out instead of doing it herself. It may now be inconvenient to shop at the supermarket with the lowest food prices. Therefore the difference between these low prices and those she must pay for the convenience of shopping after work may have to be included. She may not have time to cook dinner or other meals as she once did. Instead of peeling potatoes and vegetables and cooking meat for a long time, she may buy prepackaged dinners, which need only to be heated but cost more.

Next, you should consider expenses connected with the job itself: bus or train fares or the cost of running a car to and from your place of employment; the cost of stylish clothing, dresses, uniforms, and the like; the cost of more frequent hairdressings and other beauty treatments. Your lunch may cost considerably more at work than it would cost at home. There will be other expenses—for the cup of coffee with bun or roll at mid-morning, for contributions to buy a present for the fellow worker who is getting married or quitting to have a baby, for drinks with your co-workers at the end of the day.

Then, too, you should consider what I call the "psychological cost" of a job, which reflects itself in extra spending. The average wife who works wants to feel that she is entitled to some extras she would be unable to afford as a housewife. She wants to indulge herself at least a little bit. She may buy more expensive shoes than she would normally get, she may pay more for beauty treatments, she may want to eat dinner at a restaurant more often.

Many young mothers, after making the kind of computation I have suggested, have concluded that they will be better off economically if they remain at home.

"Does this mean that there is no way out for the young mother whose husband's income is inadequate?"

Indeed, there is a way out. Hundreds of thousands of young mothers solve the problems by doing part-time work that does not take them from their children for long periods of the day, does not involve much additional "job-related expense," and yet provides extra money to ease their financial strains.

After figuring what it would cost to hire someone to care for her children, a young mother exclaimed, "Why, I could make more money taking care of other children myself!" She decided to set up a nursery for the children of working mothers in her home. This arrangement is not only profitable, it allows her to provide day-in, day-out care for her own children and gives her the satisfaction of helping other mothers as well. Some young mothers take part-time jobs as waitresses for a few hours a day, serving at the dinner hour, when their own husbands are home and able to care for their children. Some do sales work from their homes, selling greeting cards, toiletries, cosmetics, vitamins, and other items in common use. One mother of a young child sells such items from door to door. She parks the baby carriage on the sidewalk as she calls upon prospects. Wives trained in office procedures often do part-time clerical work, typing, or bookkeeping in their homes.

If your children are of school age, you might obtain a sales position at a local department store, arranging your working hours so that you will be on duty when they are at school. One mother of an eight-year-old drops her child off at elementary school, proceeds to a nearby dress shop, works from 9:30 A.M. to 3:00 P.M., then picks up her child on her way home. The youngster of course does not miss his mother, and she avoids the expense of paying to have him cared for. Mothers with a college degree may find teaching jobs or other work at schools so that their working hours will be those when their children are at school.

Many supermarkets need grocery checkers to work part-time. A typical chain needs checkers for Thursday and Friday evenings and all day Saturday. Many mothers work then, while their husbands are home to care for their children. One survey showed that of all cashiers in stores, movie theaters, restaurants, and similar enterprises, one in five was a part-time employee. Sometimes factories and other industries hire women to work part-time, as do laundries. Because there is such a shortage of full-time nurses, anyone with training in this field can easily obtain part-time employment. Opportunities also exist for part-time writers (for instance, you might become a correspondent for your local newspaper by supplying stories about your neighborhood) as well as designers, entertainers, photographers, and so on.

"In my home, my father had a good income, but my parents were always squabbling about money, and we never seemed to have a cent for important things like education and proper medical care. I swore that I would give my children proper training so that they would never have bill collectors hounding them and threatening to garnishee their salaries. How can I give my children good, sound attitudes about handling money?"

This question came from a wife, thirty, with children aged eight and six. It shows a good understanding of the way we all get our ideas about earning, spending, and saving money. Like most of our attitudes about life, our ideas about money are formed in childhood, from observing how our parents dealt with their financial problems. If we think that they were wise in their management of money, we tend to spend and save in much the same ways as they did. If we think that they did a bad job in some way or other, we may do just the opposite. But however we think about this subject, our parents' examples are crucial.

How your children handle money will reflect what they see happening at home. Ideally, they should see money put in its place. If you give them the impression that money values are all-important—that a person with a great deal of wealth is automatically better than one with little or none—you can be sure that they will get your message. In most instances, they will go through life judging people by the clothes they wear, the houses they live in, and the cars they drive, rather than by any basic qualities of character. If you believe, as some parents do, that money problems should never be spoken of before the children, they may grow up ignorant of the ordinary processes of saving and spending. Some newlyweds have even asked me to explain what a checking account is all about. Although their own parents had checking accounts, they never told their children anything about the procedures for maintaining them.

You will affect your children's attitudes toward money even if you never say a thing about it; they will be watching you always, noticing whether you think carefully, compare prices, and study labels before buying anything; whether you operate on a budget and adhere to it; whether you often let yourself go and spend on things that suddenly appeal to you; whether you and your spouse consult on major purchases, or whether you each go your separate ways; whether, as one teen-age girl said of her parents, you "spend first and think later."

Because children generally get their ideas about money from their parents, it is no surprise to find that among some families you can trace from generation to generation the idea that the most important things money can be spent on are health and education and that no sacrifice is too great to give children as much schooling as they want. In other families, the tradition continues from generation to generation that money is made to give pleasure, that having a "good time" is the greatest value.

In addition to giving your child good examples, you should also teach him how to use this tool of money, just as a father might teach his son how to use a hammer and saw and a mother might teach her daughter how to use a needle and thread.

"How can I teach good money-handling techniques?"

I would suggest that as soon as your child is old enough to tell the difference between coins, you give him a regular allowance to use as he deems fit. Handling pennies, nickels, dimes, and quarters of his own, he will get to know the value of these coins. Being able to spend his allowance as he wishes, he will come to learn to make choices. He will soon realize that if he spends for one thing, he will be unable to buy something else. I would give him this allowance regularly whether he is "good" or "bad." Otherwise you might give him the false idea that those who have a great deal of money are automatically good while the poor are automatically bad.

I would also let children earn money of their own as soon as they can. Being able to earn money gives a child a sense of self-satisfaction. He feels that he is growing up and doing something adults do. He also learns that money does not reach one automatically but must be worked for in some fashion. When a child spends several hours mowing the lawn, scrubbing floors, or doing other chores for wages, he has a greater appreciation of the value of what he has earned. He is less likely to spend it on trivialities and more likely to weigh the real worth of whatever he spends it on. Of course, your child will make many mistakes, but these will also teach him something that he might not learn in any other way, so that even his errors will prove worthwhile.

In financial matters as well as everything else, example is the best teacher. Your child can best learn about budgeting, using a certain part of his allowance for saving, by seeing how you do it. He will learn about the stock market by seeing how you yourself invest and by holding his own shares, however few, in a particular corporation or mutual fund. For instance, if you give him some shares of stock when he is old enough to read, you are likely to find him looking at the financial pages of your newspaper more often than he would ordinarily. He also can learn more about compound interest by having a savings account and seeing how his money grows, little by little.

I think that you should also allow your child to take some part in family discussions about money. He should be able to see how you arrive at financial decisions, observing the factors you consider, for example, in deciding whether you will rent a lakeside cottage one summer or use the money to modernize your kitchen. It helps a child's training to know that all through life money management will involve making choices.

In participating in family discussions, he will absorb much important information about how mortgages are made and paid off, how a checking account operates, how telephone, heat, gas, and other utility bills are paid. A child exposed to such experiences will not think—as some do—that electricity comes free and that it makes no difference whether lights are turned off when they are not needed.

One of the strangest things I know of is the way schools spend countless hours teaching children forms of advanced mathematics, which most will never have to use, but fail to teach the simple principles of money management children will need every day of their lives. Usually it is entirely up to parents to see that their children learn such things as setting up a budget, getting the most for their money when they shop, using banking facilities in the most effective way, and so on. One mother told me that she did not think it was "nice" to talk to her children about money and that they would have to find out for themselves how much trouble and effort are required to earn, spend, and save it successfully. Unfortunately, her type is more numerous than you would imagine. I do not know what they expect to happen when their children suddenly find that they must make their own way in life and support families of their own. Of this I am sure: if more parents made a conscientious effort to teach the principles of good money management to their children, there would be a more solid understanding of the subject among members of the generation now growing up.

SIX What Everyone Should Know About Insurance

"We have four children, and my husband supports all of us. He thinks all our insurance should be on his life, but I think it should be divided equally between him and me so he could afford a housekeeper if I died. In a situation like ours, who should be insured?"

Life insurance is designed to provide financial compensation in case of death, to replace, at least partly, the income the family needs to survive. If the loss of a person's life will not affect the economic conditions of his survivors in any substantial way, there is no real point in insuring him. For this reason, insuring the lives of children does not make much sense. Their loss would cause you emotional suffering, but getting cash as a result of their deaths would not compensate for it. In other words, the policy should always be on the wage earner.

In circumstances such as those mentioned above, the death of the wife would be a great emotional blow to her husband and children, but it would not be nearly so great a financial blow as if the husband died, for then the family would lose its source of income. True, if the wife died, the survivors might have to tighten their belts and give up some luxuries to pay someone to care for the children, but this sacrifice would be a great deal less than the ones they would have to make if the family's income were to stop. So my advice is to buy as much insurance on the breadwinner's life as you can afford, to compensate you for the decrease in income resulting from his death.

Sometimes newlyweds seek my advice on a life insurance program. Some think it is a necessity for them. Others want it because it would be "nice" to have. However, if they are childless, the wife presumably could remarry or continue to work and would suffer no substantial financial loss if her husband died. If the wife died, the husband's earning power would not be affected either. So I usually tell such couples that the need for insurance should depend on the family's circumstances and that the time to think of greater insurance is when a child enters the picture and they have the responsibility of seeing that he receives good care and attention and a suitable education. With every child, there should be an increase in insurance. As the father's income grows, his insurance coverage should grow as well.

"I earn $11,000 a year and have about $2,000 in savings. My wife and I have two children, aged four and six. How much insurance should I carry on my life?"

The answer to this question depends upon your wife's ability to work and provide some income if you die. I think that this particular father should carry at least $50,000 worth of insurance. This should be enough to allow his wife to live on the present scale for ten years or so. Her costs of living would naturally be lower, because her husband's expenses would be eliminated. Too, as a widow with dependent children she will probably be entitled to Social Security payments. Taking into consideration the fact that the insurance payment will earn some interest, it might be possible for her to keep going at her present level for ten to fifteen years. By taking a part-time job, she might have enough to sustain her in reasonable comfort until the children graduate from high school and can contribute to their own support. Nor should the possibility that she might remarry eventually be overlooked. Most young widows do.

"I need insurance on lots of things—my life, my car, my house,

my health, and so on. But I can't understand how the small premiums I pay will give me all the benefits the insurance companies promise. How can they promise to pay $10,000 if I die, when the insurance only costs me $80.00 a year? Isn't there a catch someplace?"

No, there is no catch—not when you deal with a reliable, well-established insurance company that knows what it is doing. Let me explain. As you know, many disasters could happen to you. You could die in an accident or from natural causes. Your house could go up in smoke. You could have an automobile accident, causing damage or death, and you could be sued for thousands of dollars. A milkman could slip on your front porch, wind up with a broken neck, and submit a bill to you for thousands more. These things could happen to you, or they could happen to your neighbor. No one knows for sure.

When we buy insurance, we are in effect saying to thousands of other people: "We know that these disasters happen and can cause tremendous financial hardship. Let's all chip in a certain amount. Then if one of these catastrophes happens to us, we or our heirs can draw on the total amount in the pool so that the financial loss will be minimized. Let's look at the statistics, find out how often these disasters happen and then assess each one of us so that there will be enough money in the pool to pay all claims in full." As a result, by paying small sums regularly, we share each others' risk. In this way, insurance makes it easier for each of us to guard against the uncertainties of life and gives us protection we could not achieve alone.

In the example I have just given, I am talking about pure insurance. It may well be that this year you will pay out several hundred dollars for life insurance and a few hundred more for automobile, hospitalization, fire, and personal liability insurance and not collect a cent from any of them. In such a case, you might consider the hundreds of dollars you have paid as "lost," but this is not so. Actually you have bought security for this sum, and the amount you have paid has been used to pay the claims of someone else who has been the victim of a calamity.

The money paid the various insurance companies is not theirs to keep, although some of it is used to pay administrative expenses, plus dividends to the shareholders if it is a stock company. Most of what they take in is used to pay others. If you have a claim at some later date, the insurance company may pay out on your behalf much more than you have put in, using the amounts contributed by others for this purpose.

"I am confused by the different kinds of life insurance policies—term, twenty-payment life, straight or ordinary life, endowment insurance, family plan policies, family income policies, and the like. Will you describe these policies and tell me which is best for me?"

I will answer the second part of your question first. The best insurance for you—and for almost everyone—is *pure* insurance. This is a term policy paying so much in the event of your death and nothing while you live. This kind of insurance provides the greatest protection per dollar of premium of any insurance you can buy. It achieves what should be your basic purpose in taking out insurance—protection. Other kinds of life policies provide this protection plus savings features, for which you pay extra. In others, you are asking the insurance companies to do your saving for you. But generally the savings in such policies pay considerably lower interest than you could get elsewhere.

To describe these different policies briefly:

Term insurance, as I have mentioned, is pure insurance. You pay so much per year for protection against death. If you die, your survivors get the full amount of the policy; if you live, you get nothing—except in a few cases, in which you get a little something—and the money you have paid in premiums is used to pay the heirs of someone else who has died. A common decreasing term policy has a provision enabling you to renew it every five or ten years without an additional medical examination. This means that you have guaranteed protection even if in the future you develop a deadly disease that would make you ineligible for a new policy. You have the privilege of converting to a lifetime policy. The amount of premiums you pay on each renewal of your policy is determined by your age when the policy is written. This means that each fixed-term policy costs more than the one preceding it. Some persons consider this a disadvantage, because at age fifty-five or sixty the cost may seem prohibitive. Under ordinary circumstances, however, the average person does not have the need for insurance at sixty that he does at thirty, because by then his children are grown-up and self-supporting and would not suffer great financial hardship from his death. If he has been a reasonably prudent saver during his life, he has already substituted the value of his policy through other means.

Other people find the fact that they may pay thousands of dollars in premiums without collecting a cent hard to accept. Since they lack confidence in their ability to save on their own or lack the know-how, they favor policies in which cash values build up year after year. What they overlook, however, is that they pay much more in premiums for these cash-value policies, that the cost of the pure insurance is deducted, and that the cash value is what is left after this deduction. Let me assure you that insurance companies cannot pay $10,000 upon the death of someone who has paid only $500 or so in premiums without taking it from amounts paid in by its living policyholders. The death benefits must come from somewhere, and that somewhere is from the premiums of other policyholders.

Straight or ordinary life insurance policies carry a fixed premium all your life. The amount of premium greater than that needed for pure insurance creates a cash value that you can borrow against or that you can collect if you give up your policy. However, as the amount of your savings increases, the amount of your actual insurance decreases. This means that if you took out a $1,000 ordinary life policy and died in its first year, the sum your heirs would collect would consist almost entirely of money from the insurance company's reserves. After thirty years or so, your policy might have a cash value of around $600. If you died then, your heirs would collect $1,000, but $600 of this would come from your savings and the other $400 from the company's reserves. In other words, as your savings grow the insurance protection decreases. The practical result is that you are now paying the same premiums for $400 worth of insurance that once bought $1,000 worth. This principle holds true in all "cash value" policies: your premium continues the same, but your protection—which is the insurance company's risk—grows less and less.

Endowment insurance policies are generally written for a specified period, such as ten, fifteen, or twenty years or more. After this time, you may take the full amount of the policy in cash or spread it out over a period of time. Premiums for this type of policy are higher than for any other kind, because the bulk of what you pay goes into savings. Therefore it provides very little insurance at all. I object strongly to endowment insurance for other reasons as well. First, most policies are written when the policyholders are young parents and need a maximum of insurance coverage. Instead, they tie their money up in savings at extremely low rates of interest. They wind up with neither an effective insurance policy nor a profitable savings program.

"Can you give me some idea of the difference in premium costs for different kinds of policies?"

Let's consider the case of a man twenty-five years old who wants $1,000 worth of protection. The rates he will have to pay will vary somewhat from company to company. For example, if the policy is taken out with what is known as a "participating company," the premium paid will be higher, but a dividend —which is actually a refund of part of the premium paid— may be paid at the end of each year, lowering the overall cost. On the other hand, a "nonparticipating" policy may have lower premium rates, but because no dividends are paid these rates may work out to be somewhat higher than in the first case. (Participating policies are sold by mutual life insurance companies; nonparticipating policies are generally sold by companies privately owned by stockholders. Some stock companies also sell participating policies.)

If this twenty-five-year-old man bought a five-year term policy, with a provision that he could renew it in every succeeding five-year period, his cost would be between $5.00 and $6.00 for the first five-year term. It would rise in each succeeding period, as I have pointed out. If he took a ten-term policy, also renewable, his rate would be between $6.50 and $7.50 per year. If he took a straight life policy, in which cash values build up, his annual premium would be between $16.00 and $20.00. A twenty-pay life policy—one in which he paid only for twenty years and then was covered the rest of his life—would cost between $28.00 and $34.00 per year. A twenty-year endowment policy, under which he would collect $1,000 after the twenty-year period, would cost between $44.00 and $50.00 per year. These figures prove that he can get more than seven times as much insurance today by buying five-year term than if he bought a twenty-year endowment policy. If he wants insurance to protect his family in case of his death, obviously he would do better to use his money to buy term insurance.

"The company I work for has a group insurance plan. Is it a good idea for me to get into this program?"

Many employers and organizations have group insurance policies on which the premium rates are the same for all—old as well as young. When a large number of persons are insured as a group under a term insurance policy, no medical examination is usually required. Thus, a person older than average, or in poor medical condition, will find that this plan offers an opportunity he might not otherwise get, and at a much lower cost. While this type of insurance is an exceptional bargain for older people, even very young ones pay a lower premium than if they buy individual policies. Another advantage of group insurance is that a person who leaves the group can usually convert his insurance to any of the more expensive forms of life policies without taking a medical examination.

To answer your question more directly: I would advise anyone in the market for life insurance to get covered under a group insurance plan if possible.

"What do you think of combination insurance plans? I have been offered a policy consisting of insurance for all five members of my family."

You would be wise to examine carefully all kinds of gimmick policies to make certain that they fit in with your needs and circumstances.

I have before me a typical policy consisting of straight life insurance of $5,000 for the husband, term insurance of $1,000 for his wife, and term insurance of $1,000 for each child. This term insurance on the lives of the children expires when they reach twenty-one unless they convert it to a permanent $5,000 policy, which they can do without taking another medical examination. Such a policy is inadequate because the important economic loss in this family would be felt if the husband died and the family income stopped. So why pay for insurance on the wife and three children when their deaths would not involve the family in serious financial loss? Moreover, as everyone knows, death rates among children are extremely low, and the insurance company is not offering much when it offers to insure their lives. When they reach the age when death rates increase, the insurance companies change the game and require that they take a policy on their own.

Another policy combines term insurance with straight life. In one such case, the term policy has a fixed premium, but the amount of coverage decreases as the insured person ages. This makes a certain amount of sense, since the need for insurance generally decreases as children grow older and the time during which they will be dependent upon their parents grows shorter. This kind of policy may be suitable for the family with growing savings that take the place of the insurance protection.

You can find policies with all sorts of arrangements and combinations. Most of them are devised strictly as sales catchers. My recommendation is to steer clear of all of them—those that contain provisions for the education of your children, the care of your dependents, and the like. If you need insurance, buy straight insurance and then devise your own savings program.

Beware especially of policies that seem to offer something for nothing. I have been connected with the insurance business all my life, and I can assure you that insurance companies do not exist to offer something for nothing. They are carefully managed organizations that make sure that you pay for what you get and that you do not get what you do not pay for. Obviously, no business can survive if it does not operate at a profit.

"What do you think of double indemnity and other 'common riders'?"

"Riders," or additional clauses, can be added to most policies, usually at an extra charge. The double-indemnity clause provides that the beneficiary of the policy will receive double its stated face value if the insured dies an accidental death. This rider is based on the assumption that an accidental death will cause greater financial hardship to the survivors than a slow, lingering one. Usually the opposite is true. Anyone who has paid medical bills recently knows that the cost of a drawn-out illness can be almost ruinous, while an accidental death comes quickly, without warning, and, if I may use the term, inexpensively. However, the double-indemnity clause does not cost much to include, and in today's world—where death by accident is common and constantly becoming more so—it seems well worth the small additional cost.

Another rider is a disability waiver of premium. This states that if you become totally disabled and unable to work for the rest of your life, your insurance will automatically be fully paid up. This provision seems to me to be worth its modest cost, because it provides the security of knowing that a permanent disablement of the wage earner will not result in compounded financial hardship.

A "disability benefit" rider provides that a specified income will be paid regularly if the insured loses his sight or limbs. I recommend this one too.

"I want to make sure that when I die my wife will not spend

all the life insurance benefits at once and be left penniless after a few years. Can I get written into my policy a clause that she will get so much per month for the rest of her life?"

Yes. When you take out a policy, and usually at any time thereafter, you can choose different settlement options. Generally you will have four options—choose one:

1. Your beneficiary can receive a lump-sum payment.
2. The settlement money can be kept with the insurance company at a specified, unvarying rate of interest until the date you name.
3. Your beneficiary can receive a guaranteed income of so much monthly, quarterly, or yearly for a specified length of time.
4. Annuity payments can be made for life or for varying periods. The amount of these annuity payments depends, naturally, upon the face value of the policy, the beneficiary's age when they begin, and other characteristics of the particular plan chosen.

"Will I be able to change beneficiaries, settlement options, and other clauses if I want to?"

You not only can, you should. It is a good idea to review your policies every year and to update them to conform to any changes in your relationships. For instance, if your child becomes old enough to support himself, he naturally will need less financial help than would aging parents dependent upon your aid.

When you name your beneficiaries and select settlement options, base your decision on existing circumstances or those you can expect in the foreseeable future. If circumstances change, you can change the clauses. After you die, however, the conditions in effect at the time of death cannot be changed. In other words, you have written an irrevocable will.

"We have just been married, and we are astonished at the different kinds of insurance a friend of ours said we should buy. In our state we must have automobile insurance, but he told us that we should have quite a bit more than we now carry. He

also mentioned half a dozen other kinds of policies, so that our heads are spinning. Is all of this insurance necessary, or is it just another racket?"

Unfortunately, it is necessary for each one of us to carry many different insurance policies in order to protect himself in the complicated modern world. Such insurance is not at all a racket. There is nothing else that you as a prudent person can do but to take out insurance, for it protects you against catastrophes and uncontrollable factors, which otherwise could wipe you out. My philosophy is: first things first, and make sure above all that you are adequately protected against the greatest economic loss.

You mentioned automobile insurance. The kind required by your state is liability insurance, which protects you if you cause an accident with your car, injuring other people, their property, or both. For example, you are driving along the street. A traffic light suddenly changes. Before you can stop at the intersection, another car starts up, and you run into it, smashing the car and seriously injuring the driver. Your liability could amount to many thousands of dollars. If you are covered by insurance, the insurer will pay all the claims against you up to the total amount of your policy and also defend you in court should your victims sue. Ordinarily, such policies have limits of $5,000 up to $100,000 to be paid for one person injured or killed, from $10,000 to $300,000 to be paid for more than one person injured or killed in the same accident, and $5,000 or more for coverage against damage of property.

I recommend that you carry liability insurance even if it is not required by your state. Otherwise, if you are involved in an accident and are sued, it will be your complete responsibility to hire a lawyer to protect yourself in court. You will also face the prospect of having substantial claims made against you that you may not be able to pay easily. If you lose the case, everything you have saved over the years could be taken from you. Therefore I urge that you carry the limit of liability your company will assume. Huge claims are continually being decided in the courts, causing great loss to those not adequately protected.

There are other forms of automobile insurance, which you could do without, if you had to. Included in this category is collision insurance, a type of coverage under which the insurer pays the cost of any damages to your car, less some specified amount, even if you yourself were responsible for them. The usual "deductible" figure is $50.00 or $100, meaning that if you damage your car, you have to pay the first $50.00 or $100 of the repair bill yourself. If you can take out a $100 deductible policy, I recommend that you do so. But the reason I do not think that this coverage is urgent is that the total loss you can suffer if you crack up your car is no more than the value of the car itself. If you smashed up a $3,000 automobile, you certainly would feel the pain, but it would be nothing like the pain you would feel if you faced a $50,000 damage suit instituted by someone you had injured. The older your car, the less you need collision insurance.

Another type of coverage—"comprehensive" coverage—will protect you if your car is stolen or if it is damaged by almost anything except collision or upset. This insurance is not terribly expensive, and if you can afford it, fine.

Medical payment insurance is the kind that will pay for medical expenses, including ambulance service, for injuries you or any of your passengers suffer as a result of an accident in your car. This coverage applies whether you are at fault or not; it can usually be bought in amounts ranging from $500 to $5,000.

Uninsured motorist coverage—compulsory in some states—insures you against personal injury caused by a motorist who has no insurance.

One kind of insurance I do consider necessary is "personal liability." It will protect you against accidents outside your car for which you might be held responsible. The range of these is unbelievable. For example, one golfer sliced his drive and hit a man working in his garden across the street from the golf course. The ball hit the man on the head, and he was laid up in the hospital for more than four months. The golfer was sued for all the bills for hospitalization and medical care, the loss of the injured man's salary, and permanent damages that allegedly resulted. The amount sought was $150,000. Fortunately, the golfer was covered by liability insurance, and he turned the case over to the insurance company to handle. It was finally settled for $20,000—and the insurer paid it all.

I could recount many other examples of accidents that "couldn't happen"—but did. A ten-year-old girl riding her bicycle down a walk ran into a little boy; he lost several teeth and suffered multiple abrasions and contusions. By the time all the dental bills were in, damages amounted to $600. An electrician called to repair a defective light switch in a Chicago couple's home slipped on the ice on the sidewalk, cracked his skull, and was laid up for months. The home-owning couple was held responsible for damages set by a court at $18,000. A couple building a house left a pile of wood and bricks in the front yard. Two boys came along to play on them. One fell and broke his arm, and his father sued the couple. Even though the accident occurred on their private property, where the boys had no business playing, a court ruled that the husband and wife were responsible for making their yard "attractive" to children and that the boy's parents were entitled to damages of $800.

In all these cases, fortunately, the defendants were covered by personal liability insurance, and the necessary payments were made by an insurance company. This kind of insurance is not expensive—as a rule of thumb; for every $1,000 of coverage, the annual premium may run about $1.00.

If you own a house, insurance that will protect your investment in case it is damaged or destroyed by fire, lightning, or other hazards is a must. This type is called homeowners' insurance. If you have a mortgage, the mortgage-holder will insist that you take out a policy large enough so that your debt can be paid even if the house is destroyed to the ground. Even if you own the house outright, you should have this insurance so that your total investment cannot be wiped out overnight. Such insurance is not expensive. For every $1,000 worth of coverage, it should not exceed $2.00 per year for the average home of common construction not located in some area where special hazards exist. Extended coverage insurance, offering protection if your house is damaged by windstorm, hail, smoke or smudge, riot and explosion, and similar hazards, such as a tree falling on your roof or a car crashing into your property, can be obtained at a slight additional cost—from $1.50 to $3.50 per $1,000 insurance per year. Some mortgage-lenders also insist that you take out decreasing-term insurance so that the mortgage will be paid off if you die.

Whether you are a homeowner or not, you need personal property insurance, which covers your possessions—furniture, clothing, sports equipment, appliances, etc.—both at home and away. Such a policy may also protect you against the theft of any of your articles abroad. A husband and wife toured Europe by car, buying expensive souvenirs as they went along. One day they parked their car, left it to go eat at a restaurant, and returned to find that it had been broken into and the contents stolen. Fortunately, they had receipts for their purchases and were able to establish their claim with the insurance company in the United States. They were reimbursed for all their losses. Incidentally, before you travel abroad, make sure that your insurance coverage will protect you against all contingencies. Some policies do not. Also notify your insurance agent whenever you go abroad.

Personal property insurance runs about $2.50 per $1,000 coverage. I recommend it, for no matter how you try to protect your possessions—even if you put iron bars in front of all your windows—it is virtually impossible to keep out burglars determined to break in. While you should do everything reasonable to secure your home against intruders, the only true security you can get is from this kind of insurance. If you do have a loss, the first thing to do is to notify the police. Otherwise you might have difficulty in collecting from the insurer.

Finally, you should be protected against the sudden calamity of serious illness or disease that may result in extensive medical and possibly hospital bills. Major medical or hospitalization insurance is now commonplace; most large companies offer it to their employees. The employer may pay the premium or deduct it from the employees' paychecks. It also is possible for individuals to purchase this insurance on their own.

The most widely used plan is Blue Cross, under which an insured person may stay at a semiprivate hospital room for a specified number of days, get a discount on his hospital bill if he must stay longer, and receive X-ray examinations, laboratory tests, and other services. Blue Cross is a nonprofit operation run for the participating hospitals.

You can get a similar plan—Blue Shield—to cover doctor bills for surgical and medical care. This insurance will pay your doctor for a wide variety of services, in some cases even visits to his office. In some areas doctors participating in this plan agree to specified payments for their services, and the insurer pays these medical costs in their entirety. In other places, high-income people may get only a certain part of the doctor's bills paid for under the Blue Shield program and must pay the remainder themselves. In still other places, Blue Shield pays a specified amount, which may or may not be what the doctor charges.

Private insurance companies also sell major medical expense insurance. I recommend this type above all others. In a typical case, these policies will pay all expenses above a specified amount, perhaps $300. This type of policy is a must because it protects you against major catastrophic illnesses, the cost of which might otherwise be ruinous. In addition, you can protect yourself against the cost of every kind of treatment by a licensed physician anywhere, but in my judgment the cost of such insurance is prohibitive.

Most people seem to find that Blue Cross and Blue Shield insurance protection is adequate. The cost of these policies varies and is continually rising, so that any prices I might mention would not be meaningful when this book is read. However, because such insurance is offered to groups and the costs of administering it are low, it probably is as inexpensive as any.

"How do I go about selecting a reliable insurance agent?"

Here is the recommendation of the Institute of Life Insurance—a recommendation I fully endorse, no matter what kind of insurance is involved:

> Find out just as you would locate a doctor or lawyer. Ask your friends if they know an agent who knows his business—one in whom you can have confidence. Keep in mind that you will deal with your agent through the years, and therefore you will want someone who will become a trusted adviser.
>
> The good agent has been given extensive training courses by his company and is carefully schooled in serving his client's needs. As a general rule, he must secure a license before he may solicit any kind of insurance. In many states he must pass a written examination before qualifying for a license.
>
> If you have a competent agent, you can depend upon him to choose a reliable company. The company also should be licensed by your state. A license means that it has complied with state laws designed to protect policyholders; is subject to regular periodic examinations by the Insurance Commissioner; has filed annual financial reports with the state; maintains required legal reserves; and has been judged as qualified to do business in the state.

SEVEN Saving for Short-Term Needs

"How large a savings account should I have?"

Behind this question lies an understandable concern—the questioner's fear of what the future will bring and his desire to protect himself as much as possible against sudden catastrophe. Persons who ask me this question well know that misfortune and accidents happen to everyone and that it is always prudent to protect oneself in case conditions of life become stormier than at present.

When people ask me about savings programs, I find that it helps to split the subject into three categories—emergency fund before anything else and then savings for short-term and long-term purposes. Short-term savings are those intended to meet emergencies that might arise at any time—an operation or illness that is not covered by your health and accident insurance policies, repairs on your house, a period of unemployment, and so on. Long-term savings are those to help you achieve your long-term goals—to obtain the down payment for a house, to finance your children in college, to provide a nest egg for retirement. As we shall see, how you should deal with short-term savings and how you should handle your long-term objectives will be quite different.

First, let us consider your emergency fund. Not many years ago, most experts in family finance agreed that from two to six months' income in a savings account would probably protect you against most calamities that were likely to happen to you. This answer was sound, considering the circumstances that prevailed when it was given. For instance, if a husband lost his job, it usually would not take more than half a year before he could get another and bring income into the home again. During the time he sought work, the savings account would cushion his family from want. If some family member required an operation, and even if medical and hospital expenses ran more than a thousand dollars, the family could meet the cost out of savings without seriously disrupting its standard of living. If the chief breadwinner of the family became seriously ill, and if under the employment conditions then prevailing his wages stopped at once, the family emergency fund would probably cover all the medical costs and also substitute for the income that had been cut off.

As you can see, the two-to-six-month suggestion was perfectly sound. Since experience had taught financial experts that few family crises lasted longer than that time, the person with six months' income in a safe place could go about his ordinary business with the security of knowing that he would not be wiped out, plunged into debt, or forced to live on bread and water if tragedy struck.

In answering the question today, I still believe that the two-to-six-month idea is valid. I believe that a family should have enough security to survive, without undue financial hardship, accidents, illnesses, or sheer bad luck of the kind I have described. But before you translate my answer on the basis of dollars and cents, you should first consider all of the built-in "security factors" you may have in your job—your union membership, your unemployment insurance, and similar things.

Let me explain what I mean. One woman came to me for financial advice, and I took her financial X ray—a questionnaire I fill out as a matter of course to enable me to get a clear picture of my client's basic circumstances. This woman said that her husband was a vice-president of a large corporation with headquarters in Chicago. He had been with his firm for eighteen years, had more than $30,000 of his own money invested in his firm's life insurance and pension plan, and was sure that his salary would continue if he became ill and remained ill for years. Even in the unlikely event that a new top management came into the corporation and began a wholesale housecleaning, causing him to lose his job, he could still expect severance pay amounting to two years' income.

In addition to all this, the woman and her husband had insurance covering the bulk of any medical and hospital expenses incurred in case of illness. To top it off, they had no existing debts. They owned a home valued at $40,000, on which the mortgage had been paid off, and had no installments debts or other short-term debts outstanding. This meant that, if necessary, they could probably get up to $25,000 in a short period of time simply by placing a mortgage on their home and by taking out a personal loan at the bank where they had done business for many years.

Clearly, this couple was well protected against all the usual calamities. Financially, they could carry on for years if necessary, without suffering undue hardship. For them a few months' income in a savings account might be a convenience but was really unnecessary, for they had sufficient protection.

At the other extreme is an acquaintance of mine who earns his living as a free-lance writer of magazine articles. He is in a profession that has been called the last haven of the rugged individualist. It has its advantages, in that he is not tied to the nine-to-five routine most of us must face and is free to work at his own time, at his own pace, and whenever he chooses. But when a magazine buys his articles, it has no further financial obligations to him. If he cannot work for any reason, his income stops, no one continues to pay his salary. If he or his family becomes ill, he must pay all the medical expenses himself, less what he might obtain from the hospital insurance policy he carries. He cannot persuade a bank to lend him money to tide him over periods of emergency because he has no regular source of income—no salary the bank could attach if he failed to make the required monthly payments. He owns a home valued at $25,000, but it already has a $20,000 mortgage on it. Unlike the corporation vice-president whose case I cited above, this free-lance writer could not borrow additional money against his home, even if he wanted to. To make matters worse, he is not even covered by the ordinary unemployment insurance and is not eligible for unemployment benefits if he can no longer sell his articles.

In view of the writer's circumstances, it is obvious that he needs a great deal more of a cushion in savings than the vice-president. He may well need more than six months' income before he can really feel secure. In fact, professional writers need as much as a year's savings to provide adequate protection against sickness, disability, or loss of income for any other reason.

Your own circumstances probably lie somewhere between the two somewhat extreme examples I have cited. Even if you seem well protected against the common disasters—illness, loss of job, etc.—emergencies requiring you to make large cash outlays are still likely to crop up. If you own a home, your furnace may suddenly conk out and have to be replaced. A heavy rainstorm may bring you face to face with the fact that you need new shingles on your roof. A parent or other close relative may become seriously ill, and you may feel it your duty to travel to the bedside to help out until he or she recovers.

Incidents like these happen so often that they might even be considered normal. The prudent money manager must always provide for them. So I would say that even if you are well protected against sudden medical bills or loss of income due to unemployment or illness, you should have at least two months' income held in reserve for these quick, unexpected demands for cash.

"Where is the best place to keep my emergency savings?"

You will want your emergency savings to give you a fixed number of dollars, readily available and easily accessible, to enable you to deal with a crisis as it arises. Therefore, your savings should be safe above all. They should also do some work for you by giving you some return while you keep them in reserve. However, don't let interest alone be the determining factor as to where you put your savings.

Some of the ideas people have about "safe" savings would be funny if they did not have such tragic endings. You might not think that in this day and age people would still stuff their life savings under mattresses because they have no faith in the safety of banks, but I can assure you that they are still doing so. Occasionally a fire or burglary occurs and wipes out someone's life savings. One couple kept thousands of dollars in a can on a shelf in their basement. Thieves found out about it somehow: good-bye, savings.

Another couple began hoarding silver dollars until they had $2,500 worth. "If the Russians invade us, we'll be able to bribe them with silver dollars," they told me solemnly.

In another case I heard about, a young man met a girl two weeks before he was drafted into the army. He decided that he wanted to marry her as soon as his army service was over, so he sent her $50.00 every month to hold for him. When he finished his army duty, he discovered that she had moved and left no forwarding address. That was four years ago, and at last reports he had not yet found her.

The place that meets the safety requirement to the best degree possible is a reputable savings institution—your commercial bank where you maintain your checking account, your local savings bank, or a credit union. Each of these institutions has specific characteristics not exactly like the others'.

"What are the different kinds of savings institutions?"

Commercial banks are "all-purpose banks" that maintain complete banking services. In addition to handling savings accounts, they provide checking accounts for individuals and businessmen; maintain safe deposit boxes; extend loans to large corporations, small businessmen, and individuals; cash payroll checks for employees of corporations that maintain accounts;

sell travelers' checks and certified money orders; and manage estates and investment accounts.

These commercial banks may be established under federal or state charter and are examined periodically by federal or state bank examiners. If the former, the bank will be known as a national bank; if the latter, as a state bank. Savings deposits are normally insured by the Federal Deposit Insurance Corporation (FDIC). Since 1934, when the FDIC was established, savings depositors in commercial banks have only rarely lost any of their savings, and then only because of dishonesty or bad management. In view of this record it seems correct to say that savings accounts in these commercial banks meet your safety requirements.

As a rule, however, the interest rates paid by these banks are not quite so high as can be obtained in some other savings institutions. One reason is that the government requires a commercial bank to keep a high percentage of its assets in the form of cash, government securities that have a ready market, and loans that can be called upon demand or within three or six months. Since it must keep so much of its assets liquid, the bank cannot put all the money deposited with it to work. Consequently, it cannot pay out interest to the extent it could if it put more of your savings to work. Moreover, commercial banks are privately owned institutions and try to provide a reasonable return to their stockholders.

Against the disadvantage of slightly lower interest rates, however, might be mentioned the fact that if you maintain your savings account where you have your checking account, safe deposit box, and other banking services, you may find it more convenient to make monthly deposits and to build savings. For example, most commercial banks will, upon request, take a specified amount out of an individual's paycheck when he deposits it each week or month and put it automatically into his savings account. Many persons find this automatic provision helpful in building a savings account.

Another advantage of having your savings at a commercial

institution is that it helps you to establish your reputation with the bank as a prudent money manager. In time of stringent credit conditions—such as existed in late 1966 and early 1967—many banks have only enough money to lend to their own established customers. Regular bank customers during money crises thus have a source of loans available to them that others do not have.

Savings and loan associations serve a more specialized function. They use the savings of their depositors to make mortgages and other real estate loans on homes and apartments and other small operations. They often operate under different labels—for instance, as savings and loan companies, cooperative banks, homestead associations, building and loan associations, and the like. Some are owned by stockholders (common stocks of the California institutions in particular have been great speculative favorites and have had an interesting up and down, roller-coaster history on Wall and LaSalle Streets). However, some are mutual institutions; that is, they are owned by those who invest their savings with them. Instead of getting "interest" on your money in such institutions you get "dividends."

Dividends from savings and loan associations are usually higher than those paid by other savings institutions. The reason can be found in the nature of their loans, most of them to home-owners at relatively high interest rates. A savings and loan institution that can lend its money to bring a return of 6 to 8 per cent obviously can pay more to savers than an institution with a large number of 5 per cent loans on its books.

Before you open an account at any savings and loan institution make absolutely certain that your savings will be insured by the Federal Savings and Loan Insurance Corporation (FSLIC). This agency was created by Congress to protect savers (up to $15,000 of their accounts) in case a savings and loan institution defaults. While the overall record of such institutions has been good, the number that has gotten in trouble over the years has not been small. The fact that an institution invests so much money in small home mortgages means that in case of a widespread depression or the shutdown of a large industry in the area it serves, many homeowners might be unable to keep up their mortgage payments. As a result the institution might find it difficult to pay out the money to savers when they demand it. The FSLIC insurance states that every insured holder will eventually be paid in cash or credited with the sum of his savings (up to $15,000) in another institution in good financial condition. However, he may not get interest on his money while he waits to be paid. Since it began operations in 1934, the FSLIC has worked effectively in protecting savings and loan associations savers, although there may be considerable inconvenience if the institution defaults.

I do not recommend that savers go to savings and loan institutions that operate under state (not federal) charters and that have state (not federal) insurance.

Savings banks are to be found mostly in the northeastern United States. They fall midway between commercial banks and savings and loan institutions as regards the services they perform. Some perform only two basic services: holding savings for depositors and making loans to borrowers. However, many offer a wide range of services: Christmas Clubs, payroll savings plans, and sales of cashier's checks and money orders. Some have safe deposit boxes available. Some sell life insurance

Savings banks operate under state laws, which specify how they must employ their assets—the ratios that may be invested in mortgages, government securities, bonds, and preferred and common stocks, and that must be kept as a cash reserve to meet sudden withdrawals. Deposits generally are also insured by government agencies, either the FDIC (which also insures savings deposits in commercial banks) or, in some instances, insurance agencies set up by the state. This insurance provides that if your savings (up to $15,000) are in jeopardy, you will be paid the full amount of your deposit in cash, or you can have the identical amount of money deposited for you in another savings bank. A clause states that the bank may require you to let it know thirty to ninety days ahead of time when you plan to withdraw your savings. However, this provision has not been enforced and is really not worth considering. As a rule, you can get your savings here—and at other savings institutions—simply by presenting your bankbook at the cashier's window.

Savings banks are mutual institutions; that is, they are owned by their depositors. While they do not have to pay dividends to stockholders, their dividend rates nevertheless are generally lower than those paid by savings and loan institutions. This is because of the restrictions the regulating agencies place on how funds may be invested. Generally, savings bank rates are higher than those paid by commercial banks.

Credit unions are organizations of individuals with a common interest, people who work in the same factory or belong to the same religious group or consumer organization. They usually exist for the purpose of lending money to members. In order to have money to lend, the credit unions need other members who save. Interest rates paid by the typical credit union are usually competitive with those of other savings institutions.

In order to borrow from a credit union, you must be a member. It is not readily apparent to me what advantage this type of organization offers over other, larger institutions. The argument is made that credit unions lend money to those who cannot obtain loans elsewhere. If this is so, then it seems to me that the risks are greater than a saver should be expected to run. On the other hand, the credit union cannot charge higher interest rates than those obtainable elsewhere, or all the "good risks" will borrow at the other places. The advantage of credit unions is that their overhead is low. Since they have no stockholders, anything earned over and above operating costs is returned to the members in one form or other. A credit union is generally just as good as the organization that sets it up and the management that runs it.

"My wife wants to put all our savings in U.S. savings bonds, while I think we should try to earn more interest by making other investments. What do you think of these bonds as an investment?"

On my radio programs, some of the more spirited moments result when listeners ask my opinion of U.S. government savings bonds. During World War II, I developed a plan for selling bonds that was adopted all over the United States, and I was responsible for the sale of many billions of dollars of these bonds. At that time, I considered them a good investment and thought it was a patriotic service to hold them.

I do not think so any longer. One reason is that the bonds have a maximum interest rate of 4.25 per cent. This is less than the rate obtainable at this time from almost any savings institution, and a full 0.75 per cent less than that offered with complete safety by savings banks. This means that the person who buys a savings bond actually gets less interest with safety than is obtainable elsewhere.

The savings bonds generally sold to the public—the Series E bonds—come in units of $25.00, $50.00, $100, $200, $500, $1,000, and $10,000. However, you pay 25 per cent less—$37.50 for the $50.00 bond, $75.00 for the $100 bond, $150 for the $200 bond, and so on. After seven years you can cash them in and obtain the amount on the face of the bond. This works out to 4.25 per cent interest. You can also cash them in at any time before the maturity date, but your yield or interest rate will be less; it is as little as nothing during the first six months, and grows gradually year by year.

Savings bonds are intended to be long-term investments; they are not basically designed to be turned in whenever someone needs spare cash to meet an emergency. Because of this factor, it is probably not correct to compare their interest rates with those obtainable from savings institutions; you should compare them with interest or dividends obtainable from other investments held a comparable length of time.

As my discussion on long-term savings in the next chapter discloses, the greatest economic factor you have to protect yourself against is inflation. In this area, savings bonds do not give adequate protection. True, the $75.00 you put into bonds today will be worth $100 seven years from now, but first of all you will have to pay taxes on the $25.00 that has built up in interest. If you are in the 25 per cent tax bracket, that means that with one hand the government will take back one-quarter of the interest it has paid with the other hand. So you are then left not with $100, but with $93.75.

The next question to ask yourself is whether the $93.75 you will get almost eight years from now will buy as much for you then as the $75.00 you hold in your hand today. With good luck —if inflation continues at the same rate it has been going since the end of World War II—in eight years you will be able to buy only as much with your $93.75 as you can now buy with $75.00. Therefore, your money will not have appreciated in buying power at all. With bad luck—if inflation becomes more acute, which is a distinct possibility in view of the rising debt, demands of labor, etc.—your reward for buying government bonds will be that you will have less purchasing power eight years from now than you have today. This is not smart investing.

"Don't we have an obligation to support our government? Shouldn't we buy savings bonds to show our faith in America?"

I believe that our government can justify our faith as investors by making sure that we will not lose when we make an investment. It makes no sense for the average person to put his hard-earned dollars into government bonds, where his purchasing power will be whittled down largely because of the policies of that government, while more sophisticated investors put their money where it will bring a fair and equitable return.

Am I being unpatriotic? Not at all. If the government wants to sell savings bonds, it should do so in a way that makes good economic sense to the people asked to buy them.

"Well, then, how can we support the government in its programs?"

The purpose of these bonds is to get money to run the various government programs. If the government needs money, all it need do is raise taxes to meet its expenses. When it does that, theoretically everyone—rich and poor—is called upon to make something roughly approximating an equal sacrifice. All citizens then carry the burden equally.

I am all in favor of supporting the government by paying my fair share of the burden. But I do not think that those who buy savings bonds should carry an undue burden, especially since they generally are least aware of the way the purchasing power of their dollars is being eroded. I believe it is a greater service to America to invest in the corporations that give employment, build up the economy, and support the government by paying additional taxes on what they earn.

"I'm not ready to learn how to save. First, I've got to learn how to stay out of debt. Will you tell me how I can do this?"

This question, asked of me by a woman in her late twenties, reflects an almost universal state of mind among young people. The benefits of the welfare state, which presumably will care for people whether they are sick, unemployed, or too old to work, have tended to lessen many persons' interest in accumulating money for a rainy day. The idea of sacrificing what they want today in order to have something that they may need later is no longer an appealing one. Many people don't care about tomorrow. They want their pleasures today, and let the government worry about them later.

Another condition of modern times is that we often are told that we should live for today and let tomorrow take care of itself. Frankly, it takes a great deal of willpower to avoid buying all the delightful products offered to us. The constant style changes in clothing, automobiles, appliances, the constant development of new models that give the impression that products a year old are now obsolete, the attractive packages specifically designed to catch your eye—all these things make it harder to keep our money in our pockets.

On top of that, there is hardly a store now that will not gladly extend instant credit. For example, I know of a young man who walked into a discount store to buy a few pairs of socks. Before he bought them, he was attracted by a huge display of suits and topcoats advertised at 40 per cent off. He then met a salesman who told him that he did not need money, that he could get his credit approved in thirty seconds. The customer left the store after spending $150 more than he had intended to spend—and his budget was shot for months. Such incidents happen often.

If you have a checking account and see something you want, all you need to do is write a check for it. You don't have enough money in the bank? Don't worry about it. If you have signed up to enjoy this convenience, the bank will automatically lend you the amount you overdraw, charging 1 to 1½ per cent a month interest, which over a period of twenty-four months could amount to up to 36 per cent added to the cost of your purchase.

I'm sure I am not telling you anything you don't know when I say it takes determination to resist all the forces trying to get you to spend more money than you think you should spend. The question of *how* to save, therefore, becomes increasingly important, because you will find ways of strengthening your will so that these appeals to spend have less effect upon you.

Almost all successful savers I know have developed some consistent method of putting money aside. After years of practice and experience, they now do it almost without thinking. They put certain sums into savings without asking themselves each time whether they should use the money for savings or for a new beauty treatment, new hat, new spring outfit, or some other purpose. They have made *one decision* to save certain amounts regularly in certain ways, and they do not question the wisdom of that basic decision again. In other words, they save automatically. They make certain to "pay themselves" before they pay anyone else.

"What do you mean by 'pay yourself first'?"

For many people, the most effective savings method employs a bit of knowledge the income tax collectors use with great enthusiasm: the knowledge that when money is taken out of your paycheck before it reaches your hands, you tend to miss it less. This is the principle that enables the government to collect income taxes at the source and to continue to raise the amount you pay for Social Security. You tend to think of your salary in terms of the amount of money written on the face of the check, and you do not feel so keenly what has been deducted. If voters received the full amount of their paychecks first, and then had to pay the taxes, it is likely that they would not view excessive government spending as calmly as they do.

You can probably easily arrange to have a certain amount deducted from your paycheck each month for savings purposes. Some persons have their check deposited each payday by their employer in their regular checking account. They then authorize the bank to deduct a certain sum and place it in a separate savings account. Other persons ask their employer to deposit a certain amount each payday in a savings institution or apply it toward the purchase of savings bonds. Some firms have employee credit unions into which they will regularly place whatever amount you specify.

"None of these systems is available to me. Is there some way I can set up my own automatic savings plan?"

A widow I know considers that she "owes" a bill to her savings account every month. While writing checks for her monthly utility bills and mortgage payment, she also writes one to her savings account. A man has a mortgage on his home with a savings and loan institution. It sends him a monthly bill to cover the cost of interest, amortization of the mortgage, and one-twelfth of his annual real estate taxes. Upon his request, it also includes a bill for $25.00. He writes one check for the total amount, but the $25.00 is put into his savings account.

Systems such as these make the saving process as painless as possible. Saving a regular sum becomes something that is done first, not last. Persons who use one of these methods have told me that they could not consistently add to their nest egg if they reversed matters and put into savings only what they had left over at the end of the month. There is a kind of law operating for most people, I have found: they can always find something to buy when they have the money readily available.

"Are there any other automatic savings programs you can recommend?"

One woman says that she has not spent a cent in a quarter of a century. Every time she receives a penny in change for anything she has bought, she puts it into a jar. When the jar is full she deposits the pennies in a savings account. She has saved hundreds of dollars this way.

A man I knew began to cough heavily. His doctor told him to stop smoking. He decided that he needed a stronger motivation than the mere desire to stay alive, so he decided to save the money he normally spent on cigarettes and use it for travel. After only two years, just by saving an average of 40 cents a day, or almost $3.00 a week, he had $300—enough to pay his plane fare on a group tour of Europe for two weeks. Incidentally, do you know what a lifetime of smoking would cost you? Fifty years, at a pack a day, amounts to more than $8,000.

My friend's experience illustrates another important point about saving. Whether it is a question of putting spare pennies in a jar or a large percentage of your earnings into a savings account, *it is most helpful to have a clear idea of what you want to do with the money.* Motivation to save will help you make a multitude of sacrifices. In my friend's case, he convinced himself that it would be highly agreeable to visit the great historical monuments of Europe he had studied about in school. The vision he had of having a wonderful time not only strengthened his desire to put the money away, it gave him added motivation to resist the temptation to smoke again.

An emergency fund is simply the first step in a well-planned savings program. You may never need the money for some sudden purpose, in which case it can be applied toward long-term goals you can look forward to with greater relish. This goal might be a home completely mortgage-free, the opportunity to provide your children with all the education they want, the opportunity to retire earlier than might otherwise be possible, or the purchase of some luxury that would vastly increase your enjoyment of life. If you can think about these positive goals and consider how much satisfaction and pleasure they will give you, it will make it considerably easier to save the money otherwise spent on the little luxuries, comforts, or conveniences of the present.

EIGHT Saving for Long-Term Goals

"What is the difference between saving for short-term needs and saving for long-term goals?"

In your short-term savings program (one set up to give you money in a hurry), the important things to consider are safety and accessibility. Because the sum you will need for an emergency will usually not be very large, the interest rate you could earn in one savings institution over another might not be great enough to affect your decision about where to keep your funds.

However, there are different considerations when you think about saving for long-term goals—for things that you will want to use your money for in ten, fifteen, or twenty years or more. Then, appreciation in value and safety are important. The larger the amount you save, the more certain you should be, first, that your savings will not lose in value over the years and, second, that your money will work for you—that it will earn additional money and increase your wealth.

"What do you mean—'putting money to work'?"

This idea of putting money to work so that it will earn more money is an essential one in our society. It is what our capitalistic system is all about. When you invest your money anywhere in our system, you have the right to expect to be paid for its use just as you have the right to be paid for labor you perform on a job.

Whenever I mention that long-term savings should be safe, meaning they should not lose any of their purchasing power and should also earn additional money because they are being put to productive use, some members of my audience invariably nod approvingly and tell themselves that the traditional savings institutions we discussed in the preceding chapter fit those specifications exactly.

You may be excused for thinking so. Hardly a day passes that I don't see an advertisement for a savings institution telling me how I can "become a millionaire" or "make my fortune" or "turn my dimes into dollars" simply by opening a savings account and making regular payments into it for twenty or thirty years. Millions of Americans have been convinced by these means that dollars left for many years in savings institutions steadily increase in value for them.

Of course, the dollars you place in accounts insured by federal agencies are safe. If you put up to $15,000 in any single account, I have no doubt in the world that when you choose to withdraw your funds, you will get back whatever you put into your account plus whatever interest your money has earned. If you deposit $10,000 today and keep your money there for ten years, and the average rate of interest is 4 per cent compounded annually, you will get back $14,916. In that respect, what the savings institutions tell you is absolutely true.

But the dollar is constantly decreasing in value. Therefore the question you must ask yourself is this: What will that $14,916 buy for you after you take it from your savings account and pay taxes on the interest it has earned? Will it buy a great deal more ten years from now than your $10,000 will buy today. If the answer is yes, then your money will have earned some money for you. But if it will not buy substantially more for you, or if it will not even buy as much as your $10,000 will buy today, then your long-term savings program will have failed. You will have lost ground financially instead of moving ahead.

How can you be so certain that the purchasing power of money is going to continue to fall over the years? When the purchasing power of money falls, it means that the dollar buys less and less year after year. Unless you can make the number of your dollars grow fast enough to offset the decreased purchasing power of each individual dollar, you will not have a solid long-term program.

I am talking about inflation. Inflation can be described as the steady erosion of the purchasing power of fixed money. We have all seen it in action. For instance, anyone who took a ten dollar bill to a market ten years ago knows perfectly well that it bought many more groceries than it will buy today. No matter how old you are, you can recall when ordinary items in common use cost considerably less than they do today. It is not necessary to go back thirty or so years ago, when a pound of coffee cost 30 cents, butter cost 25 cents, a large soft drink from a vending machine cost a nickel, cigarettes cost 15 cents a pack, one could enjoy a good meal in a good restaurant with wine for $1.00, and a new Chevrolet or Ford could be bought for around $500.

To give you an idea of the way inflation has cut down on the purchasing power of fixed money over the years, a dollar in the days of President Washington bought one hundred times as much as it will today. The dollar of President Lincoln's time is worth only 11 cents in purchasing power today. Twenty-three cents in the year 1900 bought as much as a dollar buys today. Many readers will remember the year 1939: for 40 cents then you got as much as you can get for a dollar today. This means, in effect, that the person who put a dollar bill under his mattress in 1939, intending to use it today, may still have the same dollar intact, and it may have been completely "safe," but its real value—its purchasing power—has been cut by more than half. What do you think your dollar will be worth ten years from now?

"What, if anything, can I do to be an effective long-term saver in today's world?"

First you must understand what inflation is doing to the purchasing power of your money, and then you must take prudent steps to make your dollars grow at a faster rate than that at which their value is being cut. If you do not do this, your experience may be like that of the couple I heard about recently. When the couple's son was born in 1950, the wife named him after her Uncle Peter. The uncle was so pleased that he opened a savings account for his namesake with $2,000. Uncle Peter had been told that a year's tuition at college with board would run about $1,500 a year and had decided that $2,000 invested at 4 per cent interest would almost pay for four years of room and board for the youngster when he was old enough to go to college.

The couple concluded that the problem of saving for their son's education was taken care of. They paid little attention to what was happening to the value of the savings account or to college costs. All they knew was that Uncle Peter had arranged for young Pete's education. You can imagine their shock, therefore, when they recently discovered that instead of enough money to pay for four years with room and board at a first-class college, there was barely enough money in the savings account to pay for one year. To be sure, the number of dollars in the savings account had grown from the original sum to $3,600. But the cost of education had grown even more spectacularly—from something like $1,500 a year to something like $3,500 a year. Present-day education costs of course reflect the factor of inflation—increased salaries for professors; increased costs of building and maintaining classrooms, science laboratories, and dormitories; and so on.

A more tragic victim of inflation is a widow I know whose husband proudly announced in 1948 that he had placed his life's savings of $100,000 dollars in a fixed annuity that would guarantee her $400 a month for as long as she lived. Four hundred dollars looked like a princely sum at that time. Based on prices then prevailing, it could have enabled his widow to live without want for the rest of her days. The husband died five years later, and the wife had only this monthly sum to live on. She continues to receive $400 every month, but month by month she sees it buying less and less. As a result of the steadily decreasing value of the dollar, she has had to move into a less expensive apartment, give up a maid she employed for years to help her with her housework, discontinue other luxuries, and even cut down on expenses she had come to consider necessities.

Millions of widows and retired people are in an even worse plight. They have had their incomes set in fixed dollars per month with the mistaken idea that it would give them security for life. In most cases, when they set up annuities, they failed to recognize that the dollar would decrease in value year after year.

"How does inflation work? What causes it?"

Fundamentally, the law of supply and demand works in determining the value of the dollar just as it determines the value of other things. We all know that if there is a great demand for a certain product, the person selling it is likely to ask a higher price than if he found it difficult to find customers. When a spectacular movie that everyone wants to see comes to town, you can be sure the price will be higher than for a film that has little or no popular appeal. When merchants are doing excellent business, they feel that they can afford to raise their prices somewhat. Or they may feel that they can lower the quality while keeping the prices the same. So inflation is, in a simple sense, higher prices. One of its basic causes is that people have more dollars to spend on goods and services than there are goods and services readily available.

Several factors can produce this condition. The first is when the government spends more money than it takes in and operates at a deficit. It throws more spending power into the economy. This money spreads out into businesses and industrial concerns, which in turn hire more workers to provide the goods or services the government wants. The government contractors also spread around the money they receive to those who supply them with raw materials, to employees, to stockholders in the form of dividends, and some of it back to the government again, as taxes. If there is not a corresponding increase in the nation's ability to produce the goods and services demanded as a result of all this spending, the law of supply and demand dictates that prices will go up.

This factor of excessive spending is one reason wars are inflationary. The government spends more on war materials and at the same time reduces the labor supply in the country by putting into the armed forces men and women who would otherwise be producing goods and services. It also requires civilians to produce munitions and other implements of war, thus reducing the number available to make goods for peaceful use. The result is a greater demand for products, fewer people to supply the demand, and higher prices.

Ideally, the amount of money a government spends should balance with what it takes from its citizens in taxes. When that happens, any extra spending the government engages in is offset by the reduction in the spending power of its citizens. The person who must pay $100 extra in taxes has $100 less with which to buy goods and services. Higher taxes reduce his purchasing power as well as some of his demands for goods and may help to keep prices from rising.

Another factor contributing to inflation is full employment—so much employment that labor becomes hard to find. Let us say that a company produces 1,000 machines of a certain type a week. Suddenly the economy heats up, and it has orders for 1,200 machines. In order to produce the extra quantity, it needs additional workers. But no workers can be found. Everybody has other jobs, and nobody needs work. The company has a choice of raising prices until it discourages its extra 200 would-be purchasers or of hiring workmen to work overtime (paying as much as one and one-half to two times the usual wage) in order to produce the machines. In this case, it is also likely to raise prices in order to cover the higher costs of production. Buyers of the machines, finding their own costs going up, consider it necessary to raise their prices. In this way, price rises spread throughout the economy, eventually touching everything we buy.

Also contributing to an upward spiral of prices is the strength of labor unions. As we all know from reading the newspapers or listening to newscasts, these unions are immensely powerful and can literally bring any basic industry in the country to a halt unless it accedes to their demands. For many reasons (not least of which is the desire of union leaders to stay in office by convincing their members that they are constantly improving wage conditions), unions seem committed to a policy of getting raises for their members every time a new contract is signed. It is true that some increases in wages and fringe benefits in union contracts are compensated for by the fact that use of improved machines and methods enables companies to turn out more goods per hour and therefore to keep the labor cost of an item in balance to some extent. Nevertheless, unions generally reach for a larger slice of the pie. Corporations pay the wage increases to keep their plants running, then invariably pass their own increased costs on to the consumer in the form of higher prices.

To discuss all the factors that create inflation would take several volumes, at least, and be much too involved for my purpose in this book. What I have tried to do is to indicate that these factors—government spending, deficit financing, full employment, the bargaining power of unions—all work together to cause prices to move up steadily, year by year.

"Inflation has been going on a long time, and I've never been so prosperous. It can't be all bad, can it?"

Almost everyone, strange to say, seems to favor a little inflation. As one economist said to me, "When I consider the alternative, how can I dislike it?" He meant that if businesses are humming, producing to near-capacity and selling as much goods as they produce, if jobs are easy to get, and if we do not have lines of unemployed, we have a happier atmosphere generally. When corporations are busy making money, the prices of their securities rise in Wall Street, and their executives and stockholders are contented. The employees also are contented, because they are working full weeks, receiving full pay envelopes, and perhaps even earning overtime. Merchants see their stores filled with customers who are not seeking out bargains or criticizing high prices, and they too are content. People feel good, and the economy is said to be "booming."

Of course, this feeling is an illusion to some extent. A workman may feel happy to have $150 in take-home pay every week when he had only $100 a few years ago. He makes this comparison and thinks he is doing better than before, and the thought makes him feel good. When he spends his income, he may not note that the suit of clothes he could buy for $50.00 a few years ago now costs $90.00. The visit to a dentist to have a cavity filled that once cost $5.00 now costs $10.00. The movie theater admission that used to cost only $1.00 now costs $2.00. You may now have a greater amount of money in your purse than ever before, but it buys no more for you than did the lesser sum a few years ago.

"Is this trend of inflation likely to be stopped in the foreseeable future?"

My answer is that there is practically no chance of this at all. Inflation has been with us in the past, is with us today, and will continue to be with us in the future. Our government is fully committed to spending programs designed to keep factories operating at full capacity and unemployment at a minimum. As soon as it sees evidence of a slowdown that would tend even remotely toward deflation (when the dollar increases in value instead of decreasing), it can be counted upon to step in and prime the pump to whatever extent it thinks necessary. We saw a good example of this in 1966, when most economic indicators pointed to a downturn in industrial activity from the feverish levels reached in the preceding years. As soon as automobile sales declined, the construction of homes, factories, and other buildings lagged, and there was a shortage of money borrowers could use to buy goods and services, the Johnson Administration marshaled forces to "turn the economy around," to encourage the feeling of prosperity that makes people feel good and helps win elections. Any future administration is likely to do the same thing.

I do not know of a responsible economist who does not think that inflation will continue. The economists agree that the house that can be built for $30,000 today will cost $40,000 or $50,000 in the not-too-distant future; that the college tuition with room and board costing $3,500 a year today will cost $5,000 or $6,000; that the basket of groceries you can get for $20.00 today will cost twice as much when today's newlyweds become grandparents.

"Even if inflation seems certain, how can we tell how much there will be?"

We can't tell exactly, but we do have some precedents to go on. In the years from 1939 to 1968, the value of the dollar dropped to approximately 40 cents. During this period, we had a wide range of conditions—some war, post-war readjustments, a period of "stable" prices, some serious national emergencies, war again in Korea and Vietnam, the space program, and then the thrust to put men on the moon. Inflation averaged about 2 per cent annually. The way things are heading, this rate is likely to be at least as great in the future as it has been in the past.

A 2 or 3 per cent annual decrease in the value of your dollars, therefore, might be considered a "normal" expectation. It probably means that you will have to earn at least 4 per cent on your money just to keep the purchasing power of your savings where it is. The reason you have to earn 4 per cent is that the government taxes any interest you earn after the first $100. At a tax rate of 25 per cent, that means that of every $4.00 you collect in interest after the first $100, you are allowed to keep only $3.00. Adding $3.00 to the $100 you had, you will be able to buy only as much a year from now as you can buy with your $100 today. And if inflation rates in the future are greater than the net amount your savings earn, *you are losing out in the battle.*

The possibility of a much greater inflationary push than now exists should not be underestimated. First, as I have said, it serves the interest of politicians to have a booming economy with full employment, and we can safely predict that the politician of the future who wants to be reelected will favor at least a little inflation. If the economy runs down while his administration is in office, he will be gravely tempted to spend and spend.

Furthermore, once the inflationary spiral starts, even in a peacetime economy, it may be hard to stop. As soon as the government seeks to impose restraints on the prices businessmen can charge for their products or on the wages working people can earn, or when it tries to increase taxes, it runs into powerful opposition. If the country gets more deeply involved in war, it is virtually certain that the value of the dollar will decline further. In 1951, during the Korean War, for example, prices rose 15 per cent. As you can readily see, the value of the dollar can drop sharply.

Some economists now consider "normal" anything up to 3 per cent increase in the cost of living a year. However, recent history teaches us that we will have periods of fluctuating inflation, in which the rate may be as low as 1 per cent or as high as 10 per cent a year. A prudent expectation, I think, would be around 3 per cent—meaning that your money, in order to earn money, must bring in that amount (plus whatever taxes you will have to pay on your gains) over a long period of time.

Obviously, your task as a prudent long-term saver is to find some method of investment that is reasonably certain of giving more than that percentage on your money.

"How can I protect myself against inflation?"

Inflation has its losers and its winners. The losers are those whose incomes are tied to what I call "fixed money." They have their funds in savings institutions, government bonds, credit unions. They will get out the same number of dollars that they put in, plus interest, but they will be lucky if all these dollars buy as much as their original sum would have bought. Other losers are likely to be those who build up large cash values in insurance policies, annuities, fixed-income bonds, and mortgages—dollars that, in effect, will be traded for a few more dollars with considerably less purchasing power. It is true that in such cases, interest or dividends will be paid on the dollars invested, but in many instances the interest will not offset the decrease in purchasing power of the dollars involved.

In other words, people who try to save for the long term in these ways will be penalized for their thrift, by inflation. That is why retired persons and widows presumably protected by fixed-dollar annuities often find that their economic condition grows worse and worse over the years. They may be able to buy steak with the value of the dollars they receive at first, but as time goes on, the dollars they get will buy no more than hamburger, then frankfurters, and, finally, hash.

Among those who profit from inflation are the long-term borrowers—those who use dollars with a certain purchasing power today and repay the lenders years later with dollars with much less buying power. One of the biggest of such borrowers is the government itself. It has been busily engaged over the years in cheapening its money, thereby making it easier to pay back its own debts and to go into debt in the future. It will go on doing this as long as people do not object to it and continue to encourage the government to spend more money than it takes in.

The way to avoid suffering from inflation, obviously, is to put your dollars where they will increase in sufficient numbers to more than offset any decrease in purchasing power. Traditional "inflation hedges"—investments that increase in value as the cost of living goes up—are real estate, common stocks, mutual funds, commodities, antiques, and diamonds. It is common for owners of homes and other real estate to sell property for more than they paid, even when they have used the property for many years. In a typical case, a man I know bought a house in 1953 for $32,000. I asked him if he would be content to sell it today for that price, considering that he has enjoyed its use for fifteen years. "Of course not," he said. "The house next door, which cost the same as mine, was sold a few weeks ago for $45,000." Tracts of land on which homes, factories, or other business buildings can be erected often appreciate in value dramatically. These sections of land, particularly those close to urban areas, generally benefit from the continuing trend away from cities into the suburbs. Land is becoming more and more precious as the number of families in the country increases. There is a steady rise in demand for houses and apartments and also for schools, churches, stores, and the like to provide the services people need.

Commodities are also a favored "inflation hedge." It takes a high degree of specialization to invest in commodities successfully. Speculators buy such items as potatoes, wheat, butter, corn, copper, and other natural resources at today's prices with the hope of selling them later when their prices have risen along with the prices of almost everything else.

Antiques and diamonds have shown a tendency over the years to follow the pattern of prices in general. In fact, persons fleeing from persecution in Hitler's Germany in the thirties often converted their assets into diamonds, which not only were easy to carry but also had a value that would protect their owners against sudden drops in the purchasing power of currency.

In our time, the most convenient way of protecting yourself against inflation is by investing in selected stocks in the corporations that are a vital part of our economy. As we have seen, the large corporations of America are closely geared to the functioning of the economy in general. If their own costs go up, and they have to pay more for the labor and materials that go into the products they make, they are generally able to pass the costs on to their consumers, keeping their profits reasonably in balance.

If you intelligently invest your dollars in a share of American industry today, you can be confident that even if inflation causes prices to double, profits will double as well, and you will be getting a return for your investment in tune with the new conditions of inflation. This is in contrast to "fixed-dollar" return, which guarantees you the same number of dollars on your money even though the dollars buy only half as much as they did when you made your investment.

In Chapter Ten, I will describe how you can invest in common stocks with the maximum of expert professional guidance and with the safety that comes with diversification.

NINE What It Really Costs to Own a House

"My husband and I and our three children live in a comfortable apartment. I often feel that I am denying my children their rights by not buying a house. Is it true that homeownership is a necessary part of successful family living?"

I receive many such questions from conscientious parents who feel guilty because they live in an apartment and like it. We sometimes get the impression that it is un-American not to be a homeowner or—if circumstances prevent us from having our own place—not to want a home. It is almost like attacking motherhood or trampling on the flag.

First, lest I be accused of being subversive, let me say that I believe people should own their own homes if they want to and if they can afford the luxury. However, I also think that they are mistaken if they believe that this is the only way for a family to live or that "buying a home is always the best financial investment you can make in your life."

Let's consider these two points in order. First, we should face the fact that not every one is the home-owning type. In order to be happy about owning a home, the average person must be able to feel a sense of security even though he has a large mortgage hanging over him. Few home-buyers can lay out the full cash price at once; they must take out a mortgage, which means that they borrow the money from a lending agency. Probably most people are comfortable about this arrangement, but some persons feel unhappy about assuming a debt that may run up to $20,000 or more and may commit them to making monthly payments for twenty years or longer.

Other persons are basically city types. They have no interest in or desire for the maintenance problems owning a home involves. Many men and women have no interest in mowing lawns, maintaining plantings, putting up and taking down storm doors and windows, tending furnaces, or making repairs around the house. They have no desire to do such things themselves, yet they may be unable or unwilling to pay a seemingly unending stream of dollars to tradesmen to do such chores.

Successful homeowners generally follow a certain psychological pattern: they are essentially home-lovers, interested in good schools for their children amid pleasant surroundings; once they arrive home from work they are inclined to want to spend their evenings in peace and rest. On the other hand, people who enjoy the diversions of the city—lectures, concerts, movies, plays, restaurants, nightclubs—might be miserable leading the suburbanite's kind of life. I recall the statement one busy career woman made on moving back to a Chicago apartment after living with her husband in a suburban home fifteen miles outside the city. "The two happiest days of my married life were the day I bought our house and the day I sold it," she said.

So don't think that you must necessarily own a home in order to give your children a good upbringing. There are many attractions for them in the city that they do not generally get in the suburbs. One important attraction is the ability to learn to go off on their own instead of having their parents escort them until they are old enough for college. At early ages, they can learn to use city buses and other transit facilities, visit museums, libraries, and other attractions on their own, visit friends when they want to, and generally take responsibility for their own coming and going, unlike suburban children, who often depend upon their parents to drive them wherever they want to go.

In some suburbs, parents drive their children on dates because the youngsters are not old enough for drivers' licenses of their own.

Against the advantages of city life, you will have to weigh the advantages of the suburbs—possibly fresher air, better schools, "safer" companions, and fewer bad examples to be seen around them, although many parents who move out of cities because there is too much "crime in the streets" have discovered that in some suburbs crime rates are increasing faster than in the cities they surround.

"Isn't a family always better off financially by buying its own house?"

The answer to this question is not nearly so clear-cut on the side of the homeownership as much propaganda would have us believe. As a rule, a square foot of living space in an apartment is cheaper to construct and maintain than one in a private house. Apartments generally utilize land more effectively, and the fact that they are usually at least several stories high means that the cost of installing essential utilities—plumbing, heating, and the like—is cheaper. Savings also are involved when one central heating system serves dozens of housing units instead of only one. The fact that maintenance men can be put on year-round salaries means that the cost of making repairs in an apartment is less per repair than in a house, where a separate specialist must be called for every job and must charge for travel time on every call. Of course, rent includes a profit on the money the owner has invested in the apartment house.

A case can be made for homeownership as an investment. A case also can be made against it. In the usual procedure, the homeowner makes monthly payments to the lending institution holding his mortgage. The payment covers taxes, interest on mortgage money, and an amount that reduces the principal of his loan so that in time he will own the house free and clear. The amounts he pays in taxes and interest are deductible, and the amount that goes toward reducing the mortgage is, in a way, forced savings. Moreover, the value of houses has risen steadily over the years in line with the inflation we have had, and the combination of land shortage due to the expanding population and continuing inflation makes it likely that the owner will be able to sell his house at a higher price than he paid for it.

On the other hand, a case against homeownership from an economic point of view can also be made. As I have pointed out, the housing cost per square foot generally is less in an apartment than in a house. Moreover, the homeowner has money invested in his house that could often be earning substantial sums for him if he invested it elsewhere. One man and woman had a $40,000 house with a $10,000 mortgage and told me that their house was cheaper than an apartment. They had all the figures assembled, but they neglected to include the earning power of their own equity, which was $30,000. Even at 6 per cent interest, this meant that their house was costing $1,800 a year more than they realized. More likely, in a systematic investment program they could earn 10 or 15 per cent on their money. Consequently, their house could be costing them as much as $375 a month more than they realized. The moral: it is of fundamental importance, when considering costs of owning and maintaining a home, to consider what your own cash investment could earn if put to work elsewhere.

A man who owned a store in the Loop in Chicago had an apartment only ten minutes from his place of business. At first glance, it seemed that he was paying excessively high rent and that he could have done better as a homeowner. He pointed out, however, that in order to buy a suitable home, he would have to invest $15,000 of his own money. He believed that investing this sum in his own business would enable him to earn an extra $3,000 a year; it also gave him added collateral, which enabled him to make bank loans with which to stock more merchandise and increase his profits even more. He figured that if he took his cash out of his business and put it into a house, he could lose up to $5,000 a year—more than his apartment cost him.

Another apartment dweller is a practicing psychologist who draws most of his patients from the metropolitan area. He is conservative to an extreme, putting his money in such places as savings and loan associations, where it earns, at this time, a mediocre 5 per cent. Nevertheless, he has sound financial reasons for living in the city. "Time for me definitely means money," he says. "If I were to commute to a suburb, I would have to allow two hours of travel time a day—time I now use to consult with patients at $20.00 per hour. The fact that I have a one-minute walk from my apartment to my consulting rooms next door instead of one hour of commuting means that I can earn $40.00 more per day, or roughly $1,000 a month. This is twice what my apartment costs me."

Renting also makes sense for a career man and woman I know who, between them, would have had to spend $70.00 per month simply for train fares to travel between their places of employment and a home in the suburbs. By applying this $70.00 toward apartment rent, they have more agreeable living quarters than they could have as homeowners.

As these examples indicate, there may be sound reasons for you to own a home, and then again there may not be. It is up to you to make up your mind about this, basing your decision on factors that apply in your own particular case. You may well decide that the advantages of homeownership—which are considerable—outweigh the disadvantages. All I ask is that you clearly understand all the pros and cons before you act, so that you will know what you are doing.

"Is there a formula that tells how much I can afford to pay for a house?"

Not so long ago, most authorities answered this question with a quick yes—the formula was from two to two and one-half times your annual income. This meant that a couple with $7,000 coming in per year could afford a house costing no more than $17,500.

To some extent, this remains a good quick guide. But so many variables are involved in the subject that you really must take paper and pencil and figure out for yourself what you can afford. Among these variables is how much cash you can put up as a down payment, how much of a mortgage you can get, how long the mortgage will run, the interest rate you will have to pay, how much your local taxes will be, how much it will cost to maintain the house, and how much it will cost the wage earner to get to his place of business every day.

Just as an example, say that two men work side by side in an office. They do identical work and are paid identical salaries —$10,000 per year. According to the formula, each could afford a house costing $25,000.

Now let us suppose that the first man, John Doe, has inherited $15,000, which he wants to use as a down payment. To cover the extra $10,000 he needs to buy the house, he can get a twenty-year mortgage at an interest rate of 6 per cent. The house is in a neighborhood with a low tax rate, and he can take a bus to his office downtown—a 25 cent ride. Let us see what his monthly expenses would be. Assuming a $10,000 mortgage at 6 per cent, his monthly payment of $71.70 would cover the interest plus a certain amount used to reduce the principal, so that the loan would be all paid off at the end of the twenty years. That $71.70, added to taxes of $960 per year, means that he would have a monthly outlay for housing of $151.70. An additional $10.00 per month will cover his cost of commuting to work.

Now let us consider the second man—Richard Roe. He has only $5,000 to put up. Consequently, his monthly payment on a $20,000 mortgage is exactly twice as much—$143.40 per month to cover interest and principal over the twenty-year period. His housing is in a district with lots of young children to be educated, and his taxes are $1,200 per year—$100 per month. Moreover, the house is in the suburbs, and he must take a train morning and evening at a monthly commuting cost (including a bus in the city) of $53.00 per month. As we can see, his total payment every month for housing and commuting totals $134.70 more than his co-worker's.

Obviously, the first man could afford a much better house than the second man, or the latter cannot afford the house he has bought. As these figures indicate, a better way to determine how much you can pay is to list the house-related expenses per month and decide for yourself whether these expenses will take too great a part of your income. This must be your own personal decision, because some people place a much higher value on living in a good home in a good neighborhood than do others. You may be the home-loving type who does not care to spend much on clothing, automobiles, theaters, nightlife, or other recreation but takes great pleasures from a home. Obviously, you could spend more of your income on housing than someone who enjoys expensive living, good clothing, expensive cars, and the like. In this world, I repeat, you must make choices, and the choices you make will determine to a large extent how easily you will be able to pay for your house.

When you decide by this method how much you can afford for a house, I would warn you to consider as income only the amount you can reasonably count on permanently each month. Don't include the income of your wife if she wants to raise a family once you move into your house. Under such circumstances, her wages are likely to cease. Nor is it prudent to count on income above your regular salary for an ordinary work week. One man had been earning an average of $50.00 a week in overtime pay for several years and had come to consider such extra work a regular thing. Suddenly the overtime ceased. He found himself in financial difficulty for several months and was obliged to take a second job in order to be able to keep up his monthly payments.

I suggest that you be conservative in determining your future income, because when you buy a house with a mortgage you are making a long-term commitment you will not find it easy to get out from under. If you have gone in over your head and housing expenses take up too large a part of your income, you may have to sell out at a loss and undergo the considerable expense of moving to a less expensive place.

"How important is it to shop for favorable mortgage terms?"

Extremely important. At any given time, it is generally possible to find one lending institution making mortgages at one-half a percentage point of interest lower than another. Over twenty years on a $20,000 mortgage, this can m ke a difference of $1,000. Another factor is that some mortgages run only ten years or even less; you can get others running up to thirty years. Generally, the longer the mortgage runs, the higher the interest rate will be and the higher the amount of mortgage you can get. If you are temporarily in difficulty, it may be worthwhile to seek a mortgage that gives you a longer period in which to repay the principal and consequently lowers the amount you must pay each month. Of course, this also means that over the longer life of the mortgage, the total you pay out for interest will be considerably greater.

Some mortgages contain prepayment clauses, by which you may pay off some specified part of the total, such as 20 per cent per year, at any time, without penalty. By enabling you to cut down your mortgage debt ahead of time, this privilege can reduce the total amount of interest you must pay on the borrowed money.

Another worthwhile feature to seek is an "open-end" clause, by which the mortgage-lender agrees to consider advancing you additional amounts in the future to bring your mortgage back to what it was at the very start, before you made any payments. Let us say you start off with a $15,000 mortgage and pay off $5,000 against it. Then you need money for improvements on your home or some other purpose. With the open-end clause, the bank may lend you another $5,000 to bring your morgage up to $15,000 again.

"What are the most important factors to consider when buying a house?"

I have asked several housing experts this question. Their unanimous answer was that the most important factor is not the house itself, but *where* it is located—the neighborhood. This answer may be surprising at first, but a little thought will convince you that it makes sense. If you had a palatial home in a run-down slum area, with factories clanging nearby and cars and trucks streaming past at all hours, it would not be very satisfactory—nor would a house, no matter how grand, in a neighborhood where you would not like the school your children would attend, where you would be dissatisfied with facilities for shopping, where the neighbors would be the kind you could not feel at ease with. On the other hand, even a poor home can be repaired and made livable if the neighborhood is one you would be happy to live in. It is easier to remodel a house than to rebuild a neighborhood. However, you are likely to find the kind of house you want in the kind of neighborhood you want. The two generally go together.

The second point is that the house should meet your own family's requirements. Surveys indicate that the greatest mistake made by young home-buyers is their failure to realize that they will outgrow their home within a few years. A typical couple bought a two-bedroom house when their first baby, a girl, was born. The house had no room for expansion. Soon after they moved in, they had a second child—a boy. A few years after that, another boy. The three children slept in one bedroom for several years, but after that the parents realized that they should separate them. They had no choice but to sell their house and move elsewhere.

Women in particular should examine a house in terms of its workability. As a housekeeper myself, I well know how many steps a woman must make in the course of a day just to keep her home in order, prepare meals, and do all the other chores that must be done. Reason suggests that she keep those steps to a minimum. For instance, a well-planned kitchen can save hundreds of steps every day. The ease with which you can bring bags of groceries to your pantry from your car in the driveway or garage is the kind of thing I would give a house points for. A well-planned kitchen should be near the dining room and should have a window overlooking the yard so that a mother can work and supervise her children's play at the same time.

The ideal arrangement for appliances enables a housewife to have refrigerator, sink, and range close to each other but with counterspace alongside each one. Sufficient storage space in or near the kitchen makes it possible to do all one's shopping in a weekly trip to the supermarket and to take advantage of timely sales. You will want to make sure that your sleeping area will not be noisy—that your children will not be kept awake at night, for example, because they can hear you, your guests, your television set, radio, or phonograph.

Many people think that quality of construction is the most important factor to consider when choosing a house. It's true that one does not want a jerry-built structure that might blow over in a heavy wind. But the experience of most homeowners has been that convenient features for everyday living—pleasant view, attractive kitchen and bathroom, playroom for the children, convenient work areas for the housewife, and so on—make living more comfortable than some solid kind of brick fortress that lacks them. I came to this conclusion myself after one woman bought a solid brick house with roof timbers and a slate roof built to last as long as the house itself. On the first wintry day after she moved in, the streets were filled with mud. There was only one entrance to the house—no back entrance, as any well-planned house should have—and through this door her three young children came, their boots tracking mud over her new carpet. "I'd trade all the brick in this house for a back door and a closet where I could get people to get rid of their muddy shoes before they tracked them all over the house," she told me.

A third point is to avoid paying too much for the house in terms of what nearby houses are worth. If you pay $50,000 for a house in a neighborhood of $20,000 ones, you may find it hard to get a good price when you try to sell it. People in a neighborhood are usually uncomfortable if the value of their house is too much out of line in either direction.

As a rule, if the price of your house is a bit below the average price of the other homes in the community, you will have the best opportunity to sell it at a profit. However, if your home is too much cheaper, it might be conspicuous, and you might be uncomfortable feeling that your neighbors look down on you. Persons to whom you try to sell the house would generally have that fear, too.

Houses, regardless of their original cost, tend to be resold at around the same general levels. This is a good thing to remember if you are tempted to undertake extensive additions that would make the total cost of your house considerably greater than that of neighboring homes. I am thinking of a couple who bought a $20,000 home in a development of $20,000 homes. The husband unexpectedly inherited some money from an aunt, and the couple went on a home-improvement spree. They built a huge addition to serve as a game room. Next they spent $6,000 on a basement-improvement project, using rare wood paneling on the walls and the most expensive floor and ceiling tile they could find. Then they added a huge swimming pool in the back yard. By the time they finished, they had $40,000 invested. After a few years, however, the husband took a job in another city, and they put their house up for sale. Prospects scoffed when they tried to get back what they had paid out, and they finally had to settle for $28,000.

The point of all these suggestions is that you should keep in mind when buying a house that: (1) you will want to satisfy your family's living needs of the moment; (2) you will want to be comfortable when your living conditions change as your family grows; and (3) you—or your heirs—will want to sell your house someday.

"All the finished houses that are suitable for our family are priced so high we can't afford them. What do you think of our building our own house and doing a great deal of the work ourselves? We are both in our twenties and reasonably handy with tools. Although we don't know much about carpentry, plumbing, or other trades, we're willing to learn."

Many people think that the only way to get a house is to have someone build it. In fact, do-it-yourself home-building is one of the oldest American traditions. The first settlers had to put up their own houses, and judging from examples still visible in many places, they did an excellent job of it.

Yes, a reasonably energetic and competent individual can save thousands of dollars by doing some of the jobs involved in home-building. Many firms specialize in providing the house components that the individual, with professional help, can erect. Sometimes a novice home-builder can hire a professional to work along with him and show him how to do certain jobs.

Some home-building jobs require muscle primarily, and other jobs call for techniques that can be learned in a day or so. Much labor is simply of the sweat variety—digging for foundations, mixing cement, laying concrete blocks, holding big pieces of lumber while they are nailed in place, and so on. Anyone with a strong back can do such jobs and in the process save the $4.00 an hour or so he might have to pay a laborer for doing them. The average male or female can, with a little training, lay asphalt, vinyl, or other composition tile floors, paint, do landscaping jobs, do rough carpentry, such as nailing subfloors and wall sheeting to be covered later, and so on. The building codes of many communities require that plumbing and electrical and heating facilities be done by licensed craftsmen, but it may even be possible to cut the cost of these contracts by paying the tradesman by the hour and serving as his helper. All in all, it is not uncommon for young couples to save many thousands of dollars on the price of a house by doing their own work on it.

I know of one couple who, soon after World War II, built a house in just this fashion. The job turned out so well that instead of moving into the house, they sold it, earning a good profit. Then they embarked on a career of buying older houses, renovating them on their evenings and weekends, and then selling them at vastly increased prices. They were able to pay cash for their sixth house. After fixing it up, they had an investment worth roughly $45,000—six years after they started with $2,000.

"We plan to sell our house and move into a larger one. What can we do to get the best price for it?"

Selling your house may well involve one of the largest transactions you will ever be involved in. The way you handle it can make a difference of hundreds and perhaps even thousands of dollars.

First, make sure that your house is in the best possible condition before you offer it. Even a few trivial details—a poorly kept lawn or shrubs, a few missing wall or roof shingles—will depress the selling price many times more than these minor repairs would cost. In fact, one real estate expert told me that a house's good exterior appearance can increase its value in the eyes of a prospective buyer by as much as 10 per cent.

Also make certain that nothing is out of order inside—that the appliances and plumbing fixtures work and the furnace is in good condition. But keep interior decorating to the minimum necessary to keep the rooms from looking shabby. Most home-seekers have their favorite color schemes and want to repaint anyway. Many women know that if the interior does not actually need painting, their husbands may object to doing it.

It is a good idea to keep your house furnished while offering it for sale. Furnishings make rooms look larger and give home-seekers a better idea of how their own furniture would look in new surroundings. That's why builders of new homes spend thousands of dollars to furnish model houses; they find it ten times easier to sell a furnished home than one in which the rooms are bare. However, a very cluttered house does not make a good impression either. It is wise to get rid of all your junk before you offer the house, particularly any in storage areas. If your closets are filled to overflowing, prospects may get the idea that there is not enough storage space in the house.

It generally is better to set a realistic price when you offer your house for sale rather than to put an extremely high one on it hoping that lightning will strike and a willing buyer will come along. An asking price that is too high scares prospects off. In many areas buyers customarily offer a lower price than the one asked, but many prospects dislike making an offer that is too far below the asking price even if their bid is much more realistic. It is better to find out what comparable houses in your neighborhood have sold for recently and to set your selling price in line with current conditions. There may be nothing wrong with asking a thousand dollars or so above what you expect to get, leaving leeway for some bargaining, but I do not recommend going much beyond that.

The time of year when you offer your house for sale may make a great difference in what you get for it. Spring and fall are the best times. The weather then is pleasant, and prospects are encouraged to get out and look around. Parents of small children are likely to want to make a decision then so that they can move in summer or early winter and get their children settled before the beginning of the first half of school in September or the second half in January. In winter, many prospective buyers will be kept home by bad weather. In summer, many will be on their vacations or too preoccupied with recreational activities to be serious home-seekers. The more people there are looking at your house, the better your chances of selling to one of them. Moreover, a prospective buyer may be more anxious to buy your house if he realizes that someone else may close a deal ahead of him.

In some sections, most homes are sold by the owners directly. In other sections, real estate brokers are often used. A broker may be able to get a faster deal for you, because he keeps up-to-date lists of persons seeking homes. Also, he is probably well informed about what your house will bring in the market and thus can tell you what would be a reasonable price to ask. He will do the work of advertising, taking prospects to your home, showing them through your house, encouraging them to bid on it, and handling all such negotiations up to the signing of the sales contract. For his services, he will want 5 or 6 per cent of the selling price. Because a broker's commission on a $25,000 house may be as much as $1,500, many homeowners try to sell their homes themselves.

Whether you are your own sales agent or employ a broker, you should have all the important details about your house at your fingertips. Prospects will want to know about taxes, cost of heating the house, monthly mortgage payments required, other costs of maintenance and operation, proximity of the nearest railroad station if one is used for commuting, nearness of schools, churches, and shopping areas, and similar details.

If you decide to sell the house yourself and bypass a broker, be prepared to advertise its availability as widely as possible. Tell your friends and neighbors, local businessmen, and others that your house is for sale. A conspicuous "for sale" sign on your lawn may attract someone seeking a home. Your local newspaper and other publications with classified advertising are also desirable places to call attention to your house. Such advertisements cost little and reach a wide variety of prospects.

You will have to be a tolerant salesman—reacting patiently if prospects arrive with little children who want to examine your bric-a-brac—and you will have to be prepared to let these strangers look through your closets.

Professional real estate brokers tell me that do-it-yourself home-sellers often try too hard to sell the house. It is better just to state the facts and let the prospect draw his own conclusions. A second mistake is to try to hide something. One woman refused to let prospective buyers look into her closets. After months of failure she gave a broker a chance to sell the house and went on a vacation. When she returned, her house was sold.

As a final piece of advice, I suggest that you not be stubborn about your price. Of course, you have an idea of the rock-bottom price you will accept, but if someone offers you a hundred dollars or so below that price, I would advise you to consider it seriously. According to surveys made on this question, you are likely to get your best offer for the house within two months after you market it. If you wait longer, holding out for the last dollar, the house may get "stale." People who might have been interested when it was offered originally seem to sense when a house has been on the market a long time and suspect that something is wrong with it. Furthermore, after a few months of failure, you will tend to become discouraged. Then you will be tempted to take a lower price than you would have taken originally, just because you have become anxious to get the house off your hands and go elsewhere.

TEN Wise Investing Needs Time and Training

"What is the difference between bonds, preferred stock, and common stock?"

The average investor who does not have special training in the field of finance generally confines himself to these three categories. A bond is basically a loan that gives the bond-holder the first claim against the company's profits and assets. The borrower agrees to pay back a fixed sum at a specified time and to pay a specified rate of interest. The loan is generally protected —if the borrowing company runs into hard times and is forced to sell out or liquidate, the lender is entitled to recover the full amount of the bond before holders of preferred or common stock get anything. If the company does not pay the interest when due, the bond-holders may go to court and obtain legal power to do whatever is necessary to protect their investment. Theoretically, you will get your money and interest whether the company prospers or not. However, you do not share in the profits.

Holders of preferred stock are entitled to receive dividends at a fixed rate and, in case the company runs into trouble, are entitled to get paid the face amount of their shares ahead of holders of common stock. Most companies with preferred stock have the legal right to hold up payment of dividends if they do not make money, but generally deferred dividends are paid later when the company again prospers. Only when a participating preferred stock is issued by the company do the stockholders get greater dividends than are called for.

Holders of common stock are part-owners of the business. They put up capital, reap the benefits if the company makes good, and take the losses if it fails. Of the three categories, common stock usually is the most speculative and the most profitable.

There are many variations of these three basic kinds of securities. Convertible bonds or preferred stock may entitle the holders to buy common stock of the issuing corporation at certain prices, so that they too can reap extra benefits when the company profits. Warrants or rights are options entitling the holders to buy common stock of a corporation at certain specified prices and times. Participating preferred stock dividends may be geared to dividends paid on the common stock—the preferred holders may get a specified fixed dividend plus extra ones as well.

"Do you recommend that the average individual become a do-it-yourself investor, or do you think he should consult an expert before investing his money?"

I never cease to be amazed at the offhand way many persons approach this business of investing in equities. I know one man who has become a millionaire the hard way—by establishing a business to make parts for the manufacturers of mobile homes. His parts business has increased in value, year by year, with the growth of the trailer industry. By working eighty- and ninety-hour weeks, he now sells millions of dollars worth of parts every year. This man has retained many of the money-saving habits he formed when he was struggling to keep his head above water. He refuses to pay more than $5.00 for a restaurant meal, it pains him to spend more than $15.00 a night for a hotel room, he wears readymade suits that he buys at discount houses, he has never spent more than $75.00 for a suit, $20.00 for shoes, or $4.00 for a shirt. Yet not long ago, he called a broker and blithely placed a buy order for 5,000 shares of stock selling for $22.00 per share—an order totaling $110,000. Later, I asked him why he invested so much in that particular stock. "A salesman of mine met the sales manager of that company and was told that the stock would double its price within a month," he told me.

"Did you try to find out why the stock should suddenly increase so much in price?"

"No, I didn't have time to look into that," he said. "I thought I had better buy the stock right away before it got out of hand."

Now, this usually level-headed man would never invest that much money in his own business without assuring himself that he could get an adequate return on his investment—in short, that it was good business. Yet he was willing to invest a vast sum in a company about which he knew virtually nothing.

My curiosity aroused, I watched the action of this particular stock thereafter. Within the next two weeks, the price rose to $27.00, and my friend felt proud of himself. Did he sell out and take his nice profit? Of course not. Then the price began to drop. The stock lost half a point one day, a quarter of a point a few days later, three-quarters of a point a few days after that. By the time this sober businessman who had turned into a wide-eyed speculator got the message that he was not going to double his money almost overnight—least of all on the basis of a hot, unverified tip—the price was down to 16. By the time he sold out, at the price he received less the commissions he had to pay on both buying and selling the stock, he had lost $45,000—more than a third of the total invested.

Do-it-yourself investors run constant risks of this kind when they succumb to the seemingly irresistible opportunity of getting in on the ground floor of a good thing. Often, the source of such tips is said to be an officer of the corporation whose stock is involved. Usually there is no way of confirming whether the officer really said what he was supposed to have said. Even if he did, my experience, and that of the others in the investment community, is that officials of most corporations often are as mystified when their stock goes up or down in price as the rest of us. Often, these officers know remarkably little about the workings of the financial community.

An engineer or sales or advertising manager may fail to appraise the development of his corporation the way a finance-minded person would do. For example, the board of directors of a company making parts for jet aircraft decided that its growth prospects for the future were good and that it should build a large new factory with automated, labor-saving machinery that would cut production costs. When this decision became known to some of the executives, they hastened to buy the corporation's stock. The price rose a point or so, then leveled off, and a year later, when the official announcement was made, was down to 60 per cent of its price.

What had happened? The "insiders" failed to realize that it would require a year to build the plant, that it would cost a great deal to move existing equipment into the plant, that production would suffer, and that profits would be cut while these changes were made. Wall Streeters saw the profits decline and decided that the company's stock was priced too high. Consequently, the price went down as well.

Later, when the company got its new plant into production and ironed out all the "bugs" such an operation entails, its profits increased, and its price went up to a point where—three years after the decision to build was made—it stood at twice what it was then. But persons who bought on the original "hot tip" had long since sold out—they were not prepared to wait the length of time it took to translate these developments into profits. They did not know the basis upon which it might be logical to buy the stock. Consequently, they got burned. So even when a basis exists for a "hot tip," unless the persons acting on it know all of the facts behind it, they may take a substantial loss anyway. Such is the hazard of investing on the basis of scanty information or letting your emotions get the better of you.

Furthermore, unless you know the facts that lead you to invest your money, uncertainty is likely to gnaw at you. I doubt that anyone but the most cold-blooded gambler can rest easy if he has placed a substantial amount in a situation about which he knows little or nothing. In my mind, this is the short road to insomnia, ulcers, and worse. There is nothing to tie your expectations to—no basis of reason or logic to comfort you, only a few words passed on from one to another. No wonder a doctor tells his middle-aged patients that if they want to add years to their lives, they should avoid speculating on the basis of tips and should stick only to situations that will enable them to sleep comfortably at night. When you invest, you should always calculate the risks.

"*How do you go about getting the information to make an intelligent investment decision?*"

For many years the New York Stock Exchange and other responsible organizations in the investment world have been advising the person who wants to buy a share of American industry to "investigate before you invest." This is excellent advice—imperative advice, in fact, for anyone who wants to have the security of knowing what is happening to his investment dollars. However, this word "investigate" covers a wealth of territory—more territory, I think, than any person with a job of his own to look after, family responsibilities, and other interests can cover. Investigating the kind of securities best suited to your particular purposes is by no means a part-time, hour-a-week proposition.

Before investigating, you must know how and what to investigate. That means you should have access to the information and techniques available to the professional. The typical modern investment analyst spends years in a university and additional years of apprenticeship in a brokerage or similar firm before he is considered experienced enough to make judgments regarding the spending of another person's hard-earned money.

First of all, he must know what to look for in a corporation. Just as a doctor spends many years in medical school and as an intern learning the signs indicating whether a patient is well or ill, so too an investment analyst must learn to detect the signs in a corporate income statement and balance sheet indicating whether or not it is doing well. Sometimes a patient walks into a doctor's office for what is intended to be a routine medical checkup and is discovered to be suffering from a grave disease. Unless the doctor knows exactly what symptoms to look for and what the symptoms mean, the disease might never be detected. So, too, some corporations that on the surface seem to be well and thriving may have internal conditions at work that will sharply cut their profitability and make them poor risks for long-term survival. On the other hand, a patient who feels terrible and has fears of deadly illnesses may be reassured by the physician that the condition is trivial and that there is "nothing to worry about." So, too, an investment analyst may be able to determine that a company in seemingly poor financial health actually has a robust constitution and will be back on its feet in no time.

It takes experience to make these judgments. For instance, you must be able to read the annual reports issued by corporations and to understand what these reports are really saying. Many people think they are reading an annual report when they scan its "capsule sum-up" and ignore the footnotes. Yet the real meat of a company's condition often can be discerned only by a careful reading of the footnotes, with special attention to what they mean and how they are phrased.

To read and understand an annual report requires a knowledge of the terms commonly used in them. You really cannot tell how well a company is doing unless you can identify such things as its book value, net quick assets, cash flow, methods of taking depreciation, net return on sales, minority interest, gross income, operating income, net income, conversion ratios of debentures, and so on. You must determine, for example, whether a company actually earned last year what it says it did —not an easy thing to do, since one company may list as expenses this year outlays that another company might spread out over a number of years. Some companies habitually understate their actual income by means of various bookkeeping devices. Other companies have a policy of overstating income in order to appear at their best before the public.

Once you have determined a company's actual financial condition, the best way to determine its value is to compare its results with those of other companies in the same general line of business. This means, in effect, that you cannot make a sound decision as to whether company A stock is a good investment unless you know that it is priced lower in relation to its earnings and future prospects than the stocks of its competitor companies, B, C, and D.

The investigating investor also has a mass of other information to digest and analyze. Once a person decides to use his own judgment in making his investment decisions, he encounters a quantity of printed matter calling for his attention that can all but overwhelm him. There are many hundreds of sources that give the impression that they can make you rich. However, once a stock becomes publicized in print, it is too late to make a good buy. One such do-it-yourself investor subscribed to several financial magazines and before long discovered that his name had been added to lists of good prospects for stock advisory services maintained by mailing houses. Every week he could count on receiving at least one and often several mailings from advisory services advertising approaches to making money in the stockmarket. It took many hours just to determine which, if any, of these services were worth consulting, and even after consulting them he would be as far from making a stock purchase as before.

The untrained person reading the mass of printed advice about stocks often becomes more confused than ever, perhaps to the extent that he cannot make an investment decision. For one thing, investment services view the stockmarket from many different angles. Some base their analyses primarily upon "technical" factors: if a particular company's stock is going well—if the charts show that it is going up in price and being bought by increasing numbers of people—some counselors may consider it a "good buy" even though its earnings or other things about it might indicate that the company's prospects were poor. Other analysts concentrate almost entirely on a company's earnings: if it is now making good profits, they may ignore its past history (when its earnings may have declined because of increased competition, technical developments, or the like). Other analysts place greater emphasis on basic fundamentals: they pay regard less to current earnings than to the underlying value of the stock itself; hence they may buy stock of a company now doing very poorly but with valuable assets, hoping that its basic resources will in time enable it to do better. Some investment advisors make their recommendations from among stocks that have made new highs for the year, on the theory that a stock will continue to move along the path it is traveling. And just to show you how confusing this business can be, other analysts have done well by making their selections from stocks selling at new low prices for the year. They look for stocks that in their opinion have gone down about as far as they will go, ones that have dropped in price because of temporary conditions having little to do with the basic value of the shares themselves. They reason that such an undervalued stock has nowhere to go but up.

The individual investor, trying to find his way through the sheer mass of investment advice he receives, is sometimes like a man lost in the jungle without a compass. Some people think the "charting" of stocks is a compass and find out to their sorrow that it is not. Unless you have a clear, concise picture in your mind of what you want your investment procedures to do for you, unless you are prepared to sift advice that fits your objectives from that which does not, and unless you have the willpower to adhere to a carefully thought out policy that will enable you to reach your objectives, you will find it all but impossible to make sense out of all the investment advice you will receive.

"Are you trying to discourage me from making my own decisions in the stockmarket?"

You're absolutely right! I do not mean that an individual cannot do well if he makes all investment decisions himself and has luck and good timing. But I do say that in order to do this, it is necessary to engage in a great deal of study, thought, and concentrated determination to keep a constant watch on what your securities are doing. Unless you are willing and able to spend considerable time, energy, thought, and money not only in selecting companies in which to invest but also in keeping an ever-watchful eye over what is happening to them, I think you would be well advised to make your investments under the guidance of qualified experts.

"Who are the qualified experts?"

First of all, they are people who have had considerable experience and training in analyzing stock values and know how to go about determining when a stock or bond represents a good value in terms of its own prospects, in relation to the prospects of the economy in general, and in relation to competitors in its field. This means that the studying of investments is a full-time occupation. And even then, with the shares of more than 30,000 American corporations available for purchase on the New York Stock Exchange, American Stock Exchange, Mid-West Stock Exchange, other regional exchanges, and "over the counter," it is impossible for anyone to keep track of even a small percentage of these corporations and what their prospects are. An investment counselor must therefore be able to draw on the resources of other organizations and to make use of the analytic information provided by other analysts, the various investment services, and the like. Before choosing an investment counseling firm, therefore, you should inquire into the background of its personnel and determine what resources they can draw on.

While past investment performance does not necessarily indicate what the future will bring, it stands to reason that a firm with a long and successful record in seeing investment recommendations increase in value for its clients is probably a better bet for the future than one with a poor record. Therefore, I recommend strongly that before you entrust your savings to a counseling organization, you determine its past performance. You can do this in various ways. Ask the other clients of the firm what results it has achieved for them. If you are thinking of taking the advice of a stockbroker or registered representative of a stock brokerage firm, you can determine through the company's literature of a few years ago what its past recommendations have been and how they have worked out.

One reason I recommend mutual funds is that the past record of each fund is an open book for all to see. You can determine how each one has performed over the years under varied market conditions and compare its record not only to the stockmarket as a whole but also to other investment funds and other investment methods. Of course, the past is not an infallible guide to the future, but it seems logical that a mutual fund management that has proved its ability to increase the value of its investments over the years has better prospects of doing it in the future than a management that has not been so successful. I will say more about this in the next chapter.

Another thing you should be sure of is the investment policy of the counselor or counseling firm—making sure that he understands what your objectives are and that he will be able to devise a program to meet them. This is a most important point. Let us say that someone has a hundred dollars a month he wants to invest in stocks, with the hope of having enough money to retire on in twenty-five years. He is earning a good income now and has no need for dividends from his stock. He is obviously interested in companies that will use their profits to expand and to make more money. As this company grows, its increased value will be reflected in the rising price of its stock. This particular investor therefore expects his gains to come from the increase in value of his stock over the years.

His investment objectives will be greatly different from those of widows who must use their money to earn money, maybe they must even draw on the principal. Obviously, they cannot afford to take the same risks the young man feels comfortable about. Nor should they invest in companies that may have good prospects but are now undergoing the pain and expense of building for the future. They need seasoned companies that will pay good dividends and protect capital, giving what they really need most of all—security.

There are many investment policies that fall within the two extremes I have cited, and a good investment counselor will tailor his or her recommendations to meet the specific needs of the individual client. Therefore, the counselor must know a great deal about you—what your basic financial condition is and most of all what you hope to achieve through your investments.

"I am doing well with my investments, but a registered representative of a brokerage firm tells me he can guarantee to make 20 per cent a year for me. Do you think anyone can deliver on a promise like that?"

In choosing a counselor or accepting investment advice, steer clear of anyone who makes extravagant promises about what can be accomplished for you. A little thought will convince you that investing in stocks and bonds is a complex procedure subject to many variables, and if one thing is sure about it, it is that nothing is sure or can be guaranteed. In view of this fact, no responsible investment advisor will make any definite promises that your investment will double in value in a year or two, or anything like that. In fact, he can make no promises. He can only hope. While you should certainly expect your money to appreciate in value, and you may make great gains, no one can make categorical statements about what can be accomplished for you.

"What kind of investment return would you consider good?"

Over the years, investment counselors have considered an average increase of 12 per cent to be a good performance indeed. Anyone who does that well year after year is doing a great deal—and I would frankly suspect anyone who promises to accomplish more than that, for he may well be promising more than he can deliver.

Let me emphasize that I do not mean that it is not possible to achieve an average appreciation of equity of greater than

12 per cent per year. What I do say is that it is something else to *promise* to do it consistently, year after year.

"What can a professional manager of security portfolios do for me?"

Such professional counselors usually represent wealthy clients and charge a specific fee depending on the services offered. In a typical case, persons investing from $25,000 to $100,000 pay 1 per cent per year on their total holdings, and those investing more than $100,000 pay one-half of 1 per cent. Many counseling firms will not accept accounts of less than $250,000 to $500,000 to start. Some managers insist on complete authority to buy and sell stocks without even consulting their clients. The investor generally receives a regular report—quarterly or semiannually—in which the manager lists the securities purchased and their current value. All costs of buying and selling the securities, taxes, etc., are charged to the client's account.

Under this method of investment, the client need not lift a finger in his own behalf, but often he does not know what is happening to his money until it is too late for him to do much about it.

In a relationship of this kind, absolute confidence in the integrity and ability of the investment management firm is of the utmost importance. You should check and doublecheck its credentials, reputation, and resources before signing up for its services. While a reputable manager usually does not handle a client's money directly (it is deposited in a bank, and the manager buys securities, pays from this bank deposit, delivers securities in their place), you should make sure that he is bonded. In this way, you will be protected up to the full amount of your investment in the unlikely event that something happens to your money or securities in the movement from brokerage firm to bank and back again.

"What are the pros and cons of fixed-dollar savings, such as savings accounts or bonds, as opposed to those, such as stocks, that fluctuate in value?"

People who say that you should keep large amounts in fixed dollars point out that you can be sure of getting back an exact number of dollars whenever you want them. In other words, if you have $5,000 in a savings account or invested in a bond, you can be sure that you will get back $5,000—or an amount reasonably close to it.

On the other hand, their argument runs, if you invest $5,000 in common stocks and you need the money for some purpose, you may be able to sell your shares for more than $5,000, but it is also possible that stock prices will have gone down and you will receive less than $5,000, thus taking a loss.

This argument makes a certain amount of sense. That is why I urge that you keep up to six months' income in emergency savings before you invest in stocks with a fluctuating value. Thus you can count on readily available money in the bank to keep going in case of a calamity such as the illness of the family wage earner, sudden hospital bills, or other emergencies. Then put the rest of your money in stocks to protect yourself against another drastic misfortune—the erosion of your capital through inflation.

A time may come when you need money and your stock happens to be selling at less than you paid for it. This is always a risk you take. In this event, you might consider borrowing against your collateral until the price of the stock rises, but always be prepared to cover your loss if more collateral is needed. However, it is more likely that you will get more than you paid—and this likelihood increases the longer you hold the stock (assuming you have made a wise choice to begin with). This is why I do not encourage anyone to invest in stocks for short-term purposes but urge them to hold on for the long pull.

Another point worth remembering is that if you have the bulk of your long-term savings in equities, it is most unlikely that you would have to sell them all at once. Let us say that you are faced with huge bills for unforeseen emergencies. These bills generally could be worked out to be paid over a period of many months, giving you time to liquidate your holdings gradually. Even if you were caught for a few months in a temporary decline in market value, it is likely that you would get higher prices when you sold the rest of your stock. Some kind of average price would be worked out, and it is entirely likely that this would be greater in terms of dollars than if you had placed your dollars where you were guaranteed a fixed number in return.

"Can you give me some simple rules for successful investing?"

I'll give you twenty!

1. Determine whether you are an investor or a speculator, and make your investment judgments accordingly.

2. Select your investment advisor carefully. Consult only someone who has knowledge, experience, and integrity—someone you are sure you can trust.

3. Read the financial and business pages of newspapers and magazines regularly.

4. Select companies that issue clear and understandable financial statements at least once a year—preferably every quarter.

5. Keep in touch by correspondence with companies in which you have invested. Ask them to explain items you do not understand or that do not satisfy you.

6. Attend stockholders' meetings whenever you can.

7. Always read your proxies carefully before signing them.

8. Consider the type, experience, and reputation of the people who manage the company in which you are going to invest.

9. First decide what industry has the greatest potential growth. Then compare the performance records of various companies in that industry.

10. Give careful thought to the salability of your holdings.

11. Don't mix your charity with your investing.

12. Don't buy unknown securities.

13. Don't buy emotionally or hastily.

14. Don't invest more than a small part of your money in promotional enterprises.

15. Don't be afraid to take a loss if you have clearly made a mistake.

16. Don't overdo diversification and spread yourself too thin.

17. Don't be afraid to ask questions of anyone with whom you do business.

18. Don't hold securities for sentimental purposes.

19. Don't buy from strangers without proper identification.

20. Don't forget that *when* you buy or sell often is as important as *what* you buy or sell.

ELEVEN Yes, You Can Become a Millionaire!

"Both my wife and I are twenty-four. We both work and earn good money, and we want to invest some of our earnings so that when we're fifty-five or so we'll be able to quit work and take life easy. Do you think our goal is realistic, and how much would we have to put aside each month to reach it?"

Many moderns make the mistake of thinking that the day of the self-made millionaire is over and that it is impossible for the average person to build a substantial fortune in his lifetime. Nothing could be further from the truth. It seems to me that it is easier for the average man and woman to become millionaires today than at any time in our history. Until recent years, it was necessary to have special skills to accumulate great wealth. Generally, you had to start your own business, working early and late and utilizing every opportunity to increase your income. Or you had to be a shrewd, do-it-yourself speculator, constantly seeking opportunities in real estate, securities, or other forms of investment. In your desire for your first million you got little help from anyone, and if you did make a fortune, almost always you could boast that you did it all yourself.

Today someone such as the young man who asked this question can accumulate a fortune so easily that I myself am astonished at the simplicity of it. It is no longer necessary to be a shrewd do-it-yourself go-getter or speculator. With the increase of professional counselors who have raised the business of investing in American industry to an art and a science, it is possible for anyone with a reasonably good income to apply a systematic investment program and build an unbelievable estate in his lifetime.

Two processes are involved: first, the regular month-in, month-out saving of a certain amount of your income; second, the regular investing of your savings in carefully selected shares of American industries. The first process I call the magic of systematic savings; the second, the magic of compound interest.

Let's take pencil and paper and prove what I mean. The young man who asked the above question told me that his income and that of his wife was $290 per week, or $15,080 per year. It was easy for them to put aside $300 every month without any strain. This was only 70 per cent of what the wife earned, and it left them with all of the husband's salary and 30 per cent of the wife's salary to live on—something they could do in comfort, without any feeling of sacrifice. We figured what the systematic saving of $300 a month would do for the couple, even if the savings never earned a cent. Three hundred dollars a month for twelve months means a total savings per year of $3,600. Assuming that this savings rate was maintained for the next thirty years—until the couple reached their objective of retiring at fifty-five—they would have saved out of income a total of $108,000, no small sum indeed.

But now let us see what those savings, when systematically invested, might accomplish. I have before me a table showing how the magic of compound interest works. Money invested at an annual compound rate of 10 per cent will double over a period of seven years. Over the thirty-year period, this couple's average saving would be $54,000—half of what it would be at the end and midway between the nothing with which they start and the $108,000 with which they finish. (In Chapter Four, you will recall, I pointed out that when regular payments are made over a period of time, the *average* amount owed is half of the total.) Now let us see what that $54,000 at 10 per cent annually would do. Over four and one-half seven-year spans, it would double roughly four and one-half times—from an average of $54,000 to $108,000 to $216,000 to $432,000 to $864,000 to $1,296,000! This would be an ample amount to enable them to retire and live comfortably, wouldn't you say? Especially since, at a 10 per cent return on the fortune, they would have an income of something on the order of $129,600 a year without touching a cent of their capital.

Of course, their capital would grow slowly at first. Their $3,600 saved the first year would earn only $360 that year. But the next year, as their capital grew, they would earn $756, as well as keeping their regular savings intact. After the third year, their total from savings plus earnings on capital would amount to $11,916; the fourth year, $16,707; fifth year, $21,977; sixth year, $27,774; seventh year, $34,151; and so on.

"Something seems wrong with these figures. Is there a catch someplace?"

Believe it or not, there is no catch. If anything, I have understated what it is possible to accomplish when you combine systematic savings with systematic investing—making use of the power of your money to earn money and letting it grow as your earnings keep earning more and more.

My arithmetic is correct, so only two things could be wrong: the ability of someone to put aside a certain amount every month over a long period and/or the ability of an investment to give the rate of return—10 per cent on a cumulative basis—that I have indicated. As to the first part, I know many people who put aside a few thousand dollars or more every year and do it painlessly. Of course, you may not find it easy to do. But it is not necessary to save so much regularly, or to do it for thirty years. A crash program, carried out over a period of a few years, may well work wonders for your financial future. Money put to work in our capitalistic society multiplies at such a rapid rate that anyone who is able through one means or another to put a substantial amount to work can literally sit back and watch it grow year after year, as long as he does not touch the capital or the interest earned.

Let me give some examples from my files. A young bride inherited $12,000 upon her father's death. She and her husband agreed that they would use it, not for current needs, but as the seed from which would grow the money to finance the children's education as well as their own retirement. They invested the $12,000, never added a penny more, and spent all of their current salaries as they received them. All the results of this program are not in, because the investment was made only eight years ago. But they already have more than $24,000 in their "nest egg" fund, and if it continues to grow at the annual compound rate of 10 per cent, in twenty years or so their original $12,000 investment, untouched, will have grown to $160,000. If they leave it intact until they are ready to retire some thirty years from now, the one simple act of investing that inheritance of $12,000 and leaving it alone will give them a total of more than $300,000. Most people would be satisfied with that.

"Yes, but where can I earn 10 per cent on my money with safety? The banks in my community pay only 5 per cent, and I don't know where anyone can get more than that."

Of course you cannot get real growth in capital from savings accounts. What I am talking about is investing in American industry—in the steel mills, automobile plants, aircraft manufacturing companies, computers, food processing, building materials, clothing, and cosmetics industries, and all the other enterprises that provide employment and basic services for the American people. I can give you the names of hundreds of good, sound, continuing industries that have, year in and year out, earned 10 per cent and more on the amounts their stockholders have invested in them. They do this because they take the risk of submitting their products to the marketplace. They stand to lose or win. But history proves that, over the long pull, these industries annually average that amount and more on their stockholders' money.

"You're talking about speculating; doesn't that mean that while I might be able to make a fortune in this way, I could also be wiped out?"

I am talking about speculating only in the sense that it means participating in the risks and opportunities of the American free-enterprise system. I am not talking about gambling, in which everything is determined by chance. I am talking about making use of your intelligence to place your funds in companies that can logically be expected to share in the growth of America. We know that investors who have taken the risks of building American industry in the past have profited tremendously, and there is every reason to believe that they will continue to do so. It is possible that some corporations now in existence will fall by the wayside within the next ten or twenty years. A few will no longer serve a function. Some others will be made obsolete by the march of technological progress. A few will be victims of poor management or plain bad luck. But the majority of the large, publicly owned businesses now in existence will still be operating ten, twenty, and more years from now, most of them continuing to prosper and to reward their investors with the profits they have made. I say this confidently because this has been the story of the American business system down through the years, and nothing I know of threatens the continuation of this trend.

"But how can I make sure that I do not invest in the corporations that fall by the wayside—in other words, that my investment will show a profit and not a loss?"

As I wrote in the preceding chapter, it is difficult for the untrained individual to select, from the thousands of companies whose shares are publicly traded, those with the best prospects for success, but, obviously, for someone trained to do so, it is possible to spot the companies most likely to succeed and those most likely to fail. Success in the business world is not a hit-or-miss thing, dependent upon chance like the turn of a card or a roll of dice. With training, one can determine which companies have the most likely prospects—either because they are in a new industry that fills a need, are exceptionally well managed, have solid financial resources, or for other reasons.

"But don't even the best-qualified investment analysts often have differences of opinion about the prospects of a stock? And isn't it true that the most successful investment analysts often make mistakes and take losses too?"

The answer to both of these questions is yes. I doubt whether anyone who has been in this business for any length of time has a perfect record or anything like it. Mistakes in judgment are bound to be made. But a way has been devised to limit the risk involved, so that even if an investment analyst makes a few mistakes, the damage will be more than offset by the gains he makes in his correct choices. This system is called "diversification." It calls for the investor to put his money not all in one particular stock, which might go sour and bring him great loss, but in a large number of stocks, in different industries, with seemingly good prospects for the future.

When you do this, you limit your potential losses considerably. The history of our economy since World War II has been such that if the shares of one particular industry or company were in the doldrums for any reason, other industries and other companies would be doing better than average. For example, while the housing industry was in poor shape in the mid-sixties and shares of construction stocks, home-builders, and manufacturers of building products were low in price, there was a boom in the shares of companies in the electronics and aerospace industries. Many such companies developed backlogs of orders that will keep them working at full capacity for years. While the automobile industry had its slump, the manufacturers of aircraft and sophisticated computers were moving ahead. Thus, when you have a diversified portfolio, the ups of one industry or company counterbalance the downs of another corporation or industry, and vice versa. An evening-out process is at work.

"If it is difficult for the average investor to select one stock with good prospects, isn't it almost impossible to select the forty,

fifty, or more he needs for the diversified portfolio that will give a sufficient margin of safety?"

Precisely. No individual who has not been trained in the business of analyzing corporations and industrial trends is capable of doing this. Probably few experts are fully qualified to do it. To make this kind of selection in a prudent and informed way requires a staff of experts.

That is why I recommend mutual funds for the investor who has neither sufficient money to create his own diversified portfolio nor the time, energy, or experience to make investment decisions for himself. The key word here is "mutual," which I define as meaning working together. A mutual fund consists of a group of people who put their money together so that it may be invested to achieve the diversification and experienced professional management that would not be possible if each one operated alone. Stated another way, a mutual fund is made up of people who have similar investment goals and pool their money to try to accomplish a specific investment purpose. Pooling the money makes it possible to spread investments over a wider number of industries and companies, thus minimizing the risk of loss if one or even several investment choices turn out to be unprofitable.

"How does a mutual fund operate?"

Let us say you got together with a group of your friends to invest in equities. You realized that you did not have the time or experience to handle your own investments wisely, so you decided to pool your savings and hire people who were professionally trained and competent in investing.

Each member would put up a specific sum—let's say $5,000. Then you would apply for a charter, draft a set of bylaws, and incorporate. Next, you and the other shareholders would elect a board of directors, which would become responsible for the results of your operation. Their job would be to hire a capable and experienced management, which in turn would be responsible for investing your money. These managers would gather the information required to make a wise purchase of preferred and common stocks and/or bonds, in conformity with the fund's stated principles. As conditions change, they might shift investments from one industry to another, from bonds to common stock or vice versa, doing whatever they considered best for the shareholders.

The board of directors would choose a bank or trust company to act as custodian, or caretaker, of all the fund's cash and securities. They also would employ a firm of certified public accountants to audit the books. As a shareholder, you would receive reports, usually every three months, telling what the management has done with your money and the condition of the entire fund. The fund itself would be free from federal income tax provided it distributed to you, the shareholders, all of each year's net taxable income and profits realized.

"Have mutual funds been in existence long enough to prove that they are a satisfactory investment form under all kinds of economic conditions?"

As of 1967, there were 3,500,000 investors in mutual funds in the United States owning $41,000,000,000 worth of shares. These shareholders represented a cross section of American life —from millionaires down to children holding as little as $50.00 worth. The mutual fund industry as we know it today is an established, stable one, dating back to 1924 in the United States. The concept has been in existence for over three centuries.

As to the future, one cannot of course predict it with absolute certainty or even guarantee that things will work out as we envision them. The future always contains elements of risk. For example, it is possible—but highly unlikely—that instead of inflation we will have deflation, and that instead of having prosperity we will have an unprecedented and prolonged depression. We could have a nuclear war, which would knock all forecasts into a cocked hat. But these possibilities seem less likely than that we will have inflation and government-inspired prosperity, because our political leaders have learned how to prime the pump and get the economy going if it begins to lag to the extent that widespread unemployment may result. The law of probability indicates that the country will continue along the course it is now traveling.

While we cannot say with certainty that investment in American industry through mutual funds will continue to provide sizable returns in the future, we can see what has happened in the past. And we can state that if past trends continue as they have, you can count on at least an average of 10 per cent appreciation per year.

When I cited these figures to a well-to-do middle-aged grandmother, she immediately bought $10,000 worth of mutual funds for each of her three small grandchildren; hopefully, they could be millionaires sometime during their lifetime.

"What factors should I consider in selecting a mutual fund?"

The reasons investors put their money in mutual funds—or in any other securities, for that matter—vary greatly. In the case I just mentioned, the grandmother was interested solely in having the investment for her grandchildren grow through the years. She was not interested in having them obtain any dividends or draw any capital gains in their childhood. Young investors with jobs and regular incomes are often not concerned about any dividends they may get; they want big capital gains to build their fortunes. Because they do not need additional income now, they can afford to take greater risks—to choose mutual funds that specifically strive for big gains but that necessarily take greater risks in the process. At the other extreme, the widow of advanced years who has no job and no prospects of income apart from what her capital can earn for her wants most of all to keep this capital secure and to get a regular, specified income from it in the form of dividends. She is not likely to care what will happen to her investments twenty-five or thirty years from now, because she will not be here to enjoy them. Since her basic interest is in protecting herself today, she will be much more conservative than young people.

Mutual funds exist to meet almost all of the usual needs of investors, from very speculative funds that make risky investments to highly conservative funds that will not enter any situation considered at all speculative. Different funds, therefore, put varying degrees of emphasis on such factors as potential capital growth, current income, and stability as shown by a proven record of earnings over the years.

Among the common types of open-end or mutual funds are:

Balanced funds. As the name implies, these funds have a balanced portfolio consisting of bonds, preferred stocks, and common stocks. Most such funds maintain at least one-quarter of their assets in defensive securities, such as bonds or preferreds, which are not likely to change very much in price and which pay regular interest or dividends. Objectives of a balanced fund are conservation of capital and income.

Stock funds. These are "fully managed stock funds." When they wish to take a defensive position, they may invest some of their assets in bonds and/or preferred stocks. When they wish to take a more aggressive position, they may put 90 or 95 per cent of their assets in common stocks. Their objective is current income and long-term growth of income and capital.

Growth funds. These have as their objective long-term growth of capital, which in turn will produce long-term growth of income. Such a fund more or less disregards stocks that may have good dividend records and concentrates on common stocks with a capital appreciation potential. Because it stresses long-term growth of capital, it may invest in some corporations that are plowing back their earnings instead of paying them out in dividends.

Specialty funds. This type of fund usually confines its investment to a single industry or region. The specialty, for example, might be in the electronics or chemical fields or in Texan or Canadian industries exclusively. Another type may have its entire portfolio in bonds or preferred stocks or even municipal bonds.

As this summary indicates, there is a type of fund for every need and objective. The prospectus of a fund, which you should examine before you buy any shares, will state its objectives and list its holdings as of the present date.

"My mutual fund says it limits its investments in common stocks to the 'legal list.' What does this mean?"

The "legal list" is a list of legal investments made by banking departments of various states and the District of Columbia. For example, the District of Columbia list consists only of those corporation shares that meet rigid requirements for stability and safety. It exists as a means of guiding trustees, guardians, executors, and administrators of estates under the jurisdiction of the United States district court for the District. If executors or estate administrators must invest funds for the benefit of widows, dependent children, or other heirs, they can do so only from this list.

To be eligible for this list in any year, utilities must have had a gross income of at least $10,000,000 per year for the three preceding years, and industrial stocks must have had gross incomes of at least $30,000,000 in each of the past three years. The companies must have earned at least 4 per cent on their invested capital in each of the preceding five years and must have paid dividends on common stock in the two preceding years and nine years of the preceding ten. The stocks must be listed, or be eligible and applying for listing, on the New York, American, Mid-West, or Philadelphia-Baltimore-Washington Stock Exchange. Investments made from this list make up what is known as a "prudent man" portfolio. The managers of funds that limit their investments to the legal list need never worry that shareholders or government supervisory agencies will accuse them of going off the deep end by investing in securities with questionable or fly-by-night characters.

"Does the government exercise any control over the way mutual funds are sold and operated? In other words, do I have any legal assurances that my investments will be made in a legal and above-board way?"

If ever an industry has come under the scrutiny of the government and been made subject to control and regulation, it is the mutual fund industry. Not only does the federal government, through the Securities and Exchange Commission (SEC), carefully examine everything the funds do—in fact, they regulate everything except the judgment of the management—every state also has explicit laws regulating their activities. As a result, every mutual fund organized under the Investment Company Act operates in what can be described as a goldfish bowl.

A fund must furnish periodic reports to the SEC and make official reports to its shareholders at least semiannually. Such reports must be audited by independent accountants. These reports show certain required material, such as gain or loss in net assets during the period under review, and usually contain a letter from an official of the fund commenting on the economic scene and the progress the fund has made or what its investment thinking at the time is.

Two important provisions of the Investment Company Act, under which mutual funds operate, are that a fund cannot invest more than 5 per cent of its total assets in any one company and cannot own more than 10 per cent of the securities of any one company. These provisions ensure built-in diversification of holdings.

"Is there any minimum amount I must invest in a fund? I have only $200 now, but I want to get started on a systematic program."

Many funds require an initial investment of only $100, and some require even less. Thereafter, you can invest as little as $25.00 a month or even less, or you can buy shares whenever you choose. In some states, mutual funds are permitted to sell contractual shares, an arrangement by which the buyer agrees to buy a specified number of shares every month or every quarter.

You can work out a number of other options, depending upon the fund. For example, you can arrange to have all dividends and other payments to you from the fund reinvested in shares, so that your number of shares will continue to increase even if you do not make additional purchases. I recommend this procedure for those who want to build capital for the future.

"Will I have to do much bookkeeping when I become a mutual fund shareholder?"

One advantage of owning shares in a mutual fund instead of in a variety of corporations is that you can keep your personal bookkeeping requirements to a minimum. Although every share of a mutual fund may represent a part ownership in a hundred or more corporations, you receive only one certificate of ownership. You need only concern yourself with the price you paid for your mutual fund shares and the price you received for them. Thus ownership of mutual funds saves you the inconvenience of recording many different stock transactions. From a bookkeeping point of view, it is probably the easiest of all ways to invest.

You will receive a personal statement from the mutual fund at the end of each year, stating how much income from dividends and any capital gains you received during the year, together with advice as to whether these payments will be considered taxable by the government and on what basis. All you need to do then is to transfer these figures to your own income tax form.

"When I want to sell my shares in a mutual fund, can I be sure of finding a buyer?"

There are two basic types of funds: "open-end" and "closed-end." Managers of an open-end fund will buy back your shares any time you want to sell them, at the price those shares are worth in the open market—the net asset value of all of the fund's investments. This net asset value is determined twice daily, when the exact current worth of all its cash, market value of securities held, and other assets is divided by the total number of shares the fund has issued. Such funds always keep some cash on hand to buy back shares, and if a large number of shareholders seek to redeem their shares at the same time, it can always sell some securities in the open market to obtain the necessary cash. Thus, you can take your money out of open-end funds almost as easily as if you had it on deposit at a bank. The net asset value of the larger open-end funds is published daily in most big-city newspapers.

On the other hand, the shares of closed-end funds are traded in the open market, either on one of the regular stock exchanges or "over the counter." The price you will get if you want to redeem these shares depends entirely upon the price someone else is willing to pay for them. This price will not necessarily be the net asset value per share. In fact, the buyer of closed-end funds generally does not pay the full asset price when he buys and usually does not get the full asset price when he sells. In some cases, however, he might pay more than the net asset price and also sell for more.

Most fund shares held by the public are of the open-end type. Investors obviously want the security of knowing that they can get the true asset value of their shares whenever they choose to sell them.

"What about the commissions you have to pay when you buy shares in an open-end mutual fund? Aren't they exorbitant?"

As I write this, the average commission runs from about 1 to 8 per cent, depending upon the size of your purchase. This means that if you have $1,000 to invest, $80.00 goes to the distributor, brokerage firm, and sales organization. This is generally the only charge you pay; you usually pay no commission when you redeem your shares. This amount represents the value of the services of the sales representative in choosing the fund that meets your particular requirements and has the best prospects of achieving your investment objectives. A good sales representative will keep in touch with you to make sure that you continue to accomplish your objectives and to advise you in case these objectives change.

For the investor who seeks the safety that comes with diversification, the cost of buying mutual funds is not appreciably more, and is sometimes less, than it costs to buy a variety of shares, all in small quantities, on a stock exchange. If an investor set out to get the diversification a mutual fund offers by buying one share of each of the thirty stocks in the Dow-Jones industrial average, he would have to pay a commission of roughly 5½ per cent. When he sold these stocks, he would have another 5½ per cent commission to pay. The total commission would run to about 11 per cent.

Another point to consider is that mutual fund shares are not intended for the "in and out" trader. You should not expect to sell for a long period of time, so that one sales commission is all you need to pay, while the value of the shares increases steadily.

A few funds charge no commission, but it is up to the individual investor to appraise their performance, since no sales representative is involved. Thus no personal service is given, and the investor is without something he vitally needs.

"Where can I get information about different mutual funds, and how do I go about buying them?"

There are now more than three hundred mutual funds to choose from, each different from the others in some way. Being different in their objectives and in their approach to the market, they have varied widely in performance over the years. The past performance of a mutual fund, like the past performance of an individual stock, is not an infallible guide to what it will do in the future, but it stands to reason that a fund's past accomplishments say a great deal about the soundness of its investment objectives and the competence of its management, and that a fund that has consistently performed well through bull markets, when prices are high generally, and bear markets, when they generally are low, will continue to do well in the future.

The best way to determine which fund will achieve the best results for you is to consult a qualified investment firm—one that specializes in mutual fund investments and has been established long enough to have a reputation in the community. It should also have recognized professional standing, as shown by its membership in the National Association of Securities Dealers. This association requires its members and their employees to pass a rigorous examination and character test.

A qualified investment counselor can determine with you what your particular investment objectives are and then select the fund that will best help you accomplish those objectives. The performance record of each fund is an open book. You can easily see what a particular fund achieved in the past, when compared to the average prices of stocks traded on the national exchanges. You can see what the particular fund has done year by year—whether its net assets value has risen or fallen, and by how much, how much it has paid out to its shareholders in the form of dividends, and what an investment in its shares made five, ten, or even more than twenty-five years ago would be worth today if all dividends and capital gains distributions were reinvested in the fund shares. This record, showing to what extent a specified amount invested years ago has increased over the years, is a basis upon which you might project what the amount you invest today will be worth ten or twenty years from now.

"I heard a speaker on the radio say that it's patriotic to invest in stocks. Don't you think this is something of an exaggeration, considering that most people buy stocks with the sole hope of financial gain?"

I don't know all the reasons any particular person invests his or her hard-earned money in equities, but I do know that without investors willing to share a stake in the future of the American industrial empire our system of free enterprise, which has given us an unequaled prosperity and made us the envy of the world, would fall to pieces. Under our capitalistic system, it is private enterprise that buys the machines, builds the factories, provides the jobs, and pays the wages of the men and women who make the products we need for our everyday existence. It has been the stimulus of this private enterprise that has enabled the American system to give our people better and more abundant foods, more and better clothing, better homes, and more of the other comforts of civilization than people have ever had anywhere else on earth. For every man employed in American factories, someone has invested $20,000 to buy the machinery, erect the factory, and provide the tools he needs to do his work. Without these investors, we would have fewer workers, fewer products to sell, and fewer things to buy. The whole of American industry would stagnate.

If you don't believe this, just look at the underdeveloped countries of the world. Many of them have raw materials that, if exploited, could enable them to achieve levels of prosperity far greater than they have ever imagined. But what has happened? Their rich people, instead of investing in their own countries, send their money outside their borders—to Switzerland, for instance—where they get a secure return from it. Many invest in American businesses. While this helps our industry, it does nothing for their own countries. As a result, many of these potentially rich nations do not even have factories to manufacture the people's basic necessities. They must buy elsewhere, and the profits flow outside their countries.

It is true, therefore, that the American investor is the backbone of the American way of life. Without him, there would not only be few jobs and much poverty, the activities of the government itself would have to be curtailed, since roughly 50 cents of every dollar of profits earned by our large corporations go back to the federal government in the form of taxes. Vast additional sums are paid out to state and local governments. Without the taxes paid by business and industry directly and the income taxes paid by the millions they employ, government would lack the money for defense, education, adequate police and fire protection, social welfare, and the countless other services we expect.

Even if the possibility of great financial gain did not exist for investors—even if they could expect only modest returns on their money—one could still argue that those able to do so have a patriotic duty to invest in industry to help the general welfare. But we do not have to appeal to American citizens to do this on patriotic grounds. The record is all too plain that those who systematically and intelligently join in building our country's future by investing in American industry often reap monetary rewards beyond their wildest expectations. That is why I say that by taking a systematic, long-term approach—by saving regularly and employing the power of compound interest so that your earnings accumulate year after year and generate new earnings—you are well on your way to making a fortune.

You may not want to make all the sacrifices that might be involved in setting $300 or $400 aside every month in order to put yourself in the millionaire's bracket in twenty-five or thirty years. You may not be able to save that much. Even if you could do so, but at great effort, you may be content instead with a fortune of $100,000, $250,000, or $500,000. But whatever your goal—even if it is a million dollars—the power of compound interest and the capacity of American industry to provide profits for its owners can put it within your grasp.

People earning ordinary incomes often ask me whether I am really serious when I say that they too can become millionaires. I invariably reply:

"Yes, you too can become a millionaire. Two things are necessary—you must have a system for doing it, and above all you must be willing to want it enough to follow your system through moments thick and thin." And these two points don't apply only to building your fortune; they are the basis of my whole philosophy concerning the successful management of your financial affairs. If you have a knowledge of how to use this tool of money and the determination to stick to your objectives no matter what the temporary sacrifice, you will be able to accomplish any goal you care to set.

INDEX

A

Accident insurance
  automobile, 106-108, 110
  personal liability, 108-109
Advertising
  bait, 61
  and impulse buying, 59
  sale of home, 155
  slanted toward women, 20
Allowance, for children, 93
Annuities, 106, 132-133, 138-139
Antiques, investment in, 139, 140
Apartments, advantages and disadvantages of, 143-145
Appliances, purchase of, 20, 53
Appreciation in purchasing power, 123, 129
Assets, 34-37, 140
  of banks, 118, 120
  loans against, 76-77
  of mutual funds, 182
Automatic savings plans, 126-128
Automobile
  cost of operating, 43, 44
  credit buying of, 78
  current value of, 37
  depreciation, 43, 53
  insurance, types of, 106-108, 110
  purchase of, 4, 20

B

Bait advertising, 61
Balance sheet, 34
Balanced funds, 182
Banks
  commercial, 117-119
  credit cards issued by, 70-71
  interest rates, 118
  loans from, 74-75, 125
  safe deposit box in, 26-27, 31
  savings, 117, 120-121
Bargains, 51, 52, 53, 56, 61
Beneficiaries, insurance, 106
Bills of sale, 24, 25, 36, 37
Blue Cross, 111

Blue Shield, 111
Board of directors, mutual fund, 179-180
Bonds, 24, 76, 157, 158-168, 182
  U.S. savings, 35, 121-124, 138
Brokers
  real estate, 35, 36, 154-155
  stockbrokers, 166
Budget, 45, 93, 94

C

Capital
  gains tax, 35-36, 38
  growth of, 175, 182
Cash
  in automobile purchase, 78
  and cash equivalents, 34
Cash value
  of insurance policies, 35, 101
  in pension plans, 35, 39
Cemetery deed, 26-27
Certificate numbers of stocks, 24
Charge accounts, 37, 64, 67, 69, 70
Checking accounts, 19, 125
Children
  city or suburban life for, 142-143
  costs of care for, 89, 90
  inheritance laws affecting, 28
  teaching money management to, 22, 91-95
Clothing, purchase of, 19, 42, 52-54
Collateral, 38, 169
  loans, 75-77
Collision insurance, 108
Commission
  on buying mutual fund shares, 186-187
  for real estate broker, 154
Commodities, investment in, 139, 140
Common stock, 139, 140, 157-158, 182, 183
Comprehensive automobile insurance, 108
Continuing credit plan, 70-71
Contract
  in installment buying, 72, 73
  loan, 77-78
Contributions
  expense of, 44, 89-90
  to pension plan by employee, 35
Corporations
  annual reports of, 162-163
  appraising development of, 160, 161-162, 170
  eligible for legal list, 183
  financial statements of, 170
  investing in, 176-179, 188-190
Costs
  of automobile operation, 43
  of child care, 89, 90
  of clothing, 42
  of contributions, 44, 89-90
  of education, 42, 66-67, 132
  of employment for mothers, 88-90
  food, 54-55
  household maintenance, 41
  housing, 41, 145-147
  of insurance premiums, 102-103

Costs (cont'd.)
of making a will, 29-30
personal care and health, 38, 42-43
production, and inflation, 134
transportation, 43, 44, 89, 145, 146
of using credit, 64-65, 71-73
Credit, 22, 63
in automobile purchase, 78
cost of using, 64-65, 71-73
and impulse buying, 59-60
instant, from stores, 124-125
long-term, 69
most economical terms for, 69-70
short-term, 69
types of, 70-77
when not to use, 68-69
when to use, 65-68
Credit cards, 59, 68, 70-71, 78-80
Credit unions, 117, 121, 126, 138

D

Debt, 13, 37-38, 39
avoiding, 124-125
Decreasing-term insurance, 100, 110
Deeds, 24
Deflation, 136, 180
Depreciation
of automobile, 43, 53
of personal possessions, 37
Diamonds, investment in, 139, 140
Disability benefit in life insurance, 105
Discount stores, 51, 124-125
Diversification of securities, 171, 178-179, 184
Dividends
from insurance company, 100
from mutual funds, 181, 182, 188
from preferred stock, 157-158
from savings banks, 121
from savings and loan associations, 119
Double-indemnity clause, 105
Down payment on home, 146

E

Easy money, 75
Education, cost of, 42, 46, 66-67, 132
Employment
expenses related to, 87, 88-89
full, and inflation, 134
group life insurance in, 25, 103
medical and hospitalization insurance, 111
outside home, for mothers, 4, 87-91
part-time, 90-91
pension plans, 24, 35, 39
records of, 26
years of, for women, 19
Endowment insurance, 100, 102, 103
Entertainment, spending for, 44
Expenditures
fixed, 41-42
records of, 41-47

Expenses
  cutting down on, 42-44, 47, 54-55
  of working mothers, 89-90
Extended coverage property insurance, 110
Extended payment plan, 71

F

Family purchases, influence of women in, 19-21
Federal Deposit Insurance Corporation, 118, 120
Federal Savings and Loan Insurance Corporation, 119-120
Finance company loans, 73-74
Finance Forum of America, The, 40
Financial institutions, 117-121
  women in, 21
Financial records
  and credit buying, 67-68, 79
  of expenditures, 41-47
  types of, 24-26
  where kept, 22-24, 26-27, 31
Financial X ray, 5, 33-49, 114
Fixed-term insurance policy, 101
Food expenses, 42, 44, 54-55

G

Galus, Henry S., 20
Garnishment, 74-75, 78
Gifts, spending for, 44
Group insurance policies, 25, 103
Growth funds, 182
Guarantees, 60

H

Home, 20
  buying, factors to consider, 148-152
  do-it-yourself building, 151-152
  how much buyer can afford, 145-147
  insurance against damage, 109-110
  mortgage on, *see* Mortgages
  owning, advantages and disadvantages, 141-145
  price of, 150-151
  selling, 151, 152-156
  taxes on, 41, 42
Hospitalization insurance, 111-112
Household maintenance, 41, 60-61, 142, 143
Housing cost, 41, 145-147

I

Impulse buying, 57-60, 79-80, 87, 124-125
Income
  annual, 40
  of corporations, 162-163
  fixed, and inflation, 132-133, 138-139
  future, determining, 147
  how spent, 22, 33, 39-40
  nonrecurring, 41

Income (cont'd.)
size of, and money management, 5-9
split between spouses, 83
Income taxes, 42, 88-89, 185
records, 26
reduction, and credit, 67-68
Inflation, 86, 180-181
causes of, 133-135
and education costs, 132
fluctuating, 138
and fixed incomes, 132-133, 138-139
future trends, 136-138
profiting from, 139
and prosperity, 135-136
protection against, 122-123, 138-140, 169
Inheritance laws, 28, 30
Installment buying, 34, 64, 65, 68, 72-73
Installment loans, 38, 74-75
Insurance, 21, 46
accident, 106-109
amount, and amount of savings, 101-102
automobile, 106-108, 110
group, 25, 103
life, 72, 97-98, 100-103
medical and hospitalization, 111-112
personal liability, 108-109
personal property, 110
premiums, 41-42, 99-103, 105
records, 24, 25
for savings deposits, 118, 119-120, 130
term, 100-101, 103, 104
unemployment, 42, 114, 116
Insurance agent, selecting, 112
Insurance policies, 41-42
cash value of, 35, 101
changing, 106
combination, 104-105
deductible clauses, 108
endowment, 100, 102, 103
fixed premiums in, 101-102
group, 25, 103
liability, 107-108
life, types of, 100-103
nonparticipating and participating, 102
premium costs for, 101-103
"riders," 105
settlement options, 106
twenty-payment life, 100, 103
Interest
compound, 94, 174-176, 190
taxes paid on, 137, 138
Interest rates
on amount overdrawn, 125
on bonds, 157
on charge accounts, 69, 70
charged by loan companies, 74
on credit, 64-65, 71, 79
on installment payments, 72-73
on loans, 75-77, 119
on mortgages, 76, 143, 146, 148
paid by commercial banks, 118
paid by credit unions, 121
on savings, 117, 130
of U.S. savings bonds, 122
Investment analyst, 161-164, 178

Investment Company Act, 184
Investment counselors, 165, 166-167, 170, 187-188
Investment management firms, 168
Investments, 22, 129-130
  diversification of, 171, 178-179, 184
Investments
  homeownership as, 143-144
  increasing in value with inflation, 139-140
  in industry, 176-179
  investigating, 161-164
  legal list of, 183
  long-term, 122, 169
  making intelligent decisions on, 161-164, 170-171
  mutual funds, 36, 139, 166, 179-188
  objectives, 164, 166, 167, 181
  qualified experts on, 165-167
  return on, 167-168
  systematic program, 174-176, 190
  types of, 157-158
  U.S. savings bonds, 35, 121-124, 138
  value to society, 188-190
  See also Bonds; Stocks

L

Legal list, 183
Liabilities, 37-38
Liability insurance, 107
  personal, 108-109
Life insurance
  on installment payment, 72
  types of, 100-103
  for wage earner, 97-98
Linens, purchase of, 53-54
Loan companies, 73-74
Loans, 36
  from banks, 74-75, 125
  bonds as, 157, 158
  collateral, 75-77
  contracts, 77-78
  interest rates on, 75-77
  from loan companies, 73-74
  mortgage, 76
  record of, 24-25, 38
  from savings and loan associations, 119
  short-term, 69-70

M

McGinnis, Tom, 83
Major medical expense insurance, 111
Market price of stocks, 36
Marriage
  financial arguments in, 81-83, 84
  inheritance laws in, 30
Meat costs, 54
Medical insurance, 111-112
Medical payment insurance, 108
Millionaire, how to become, 173-190
Money
  "easy" and "tight," 75
  fixed, effect of inflation on purchasing power, 132-133, 138-139
  uses of, 1-3

Money management
attitudes toward, 9-10, 11, 48-49, 84-86, 91-93
causes of difficulty in, 5, 10, 12-14, 57-60, 83-87
competence in, 22-27
decisions in, 3-5, 6-9, 15-16, 60, 93, 94
how to begin, 33
marital arguments over, 81-83, 84
philosophy of, 190
role of each spouse, 83-84
role of women in, 17-19, 21-22, 82, 84
and size of income, 5-9
teaching to children, 22, 91-95
in widowhood, 18
Mortgages, 24, 38, 41, 42, 66, 69, 75-76, 141-142, 147
insurance to cover, 109, 110
interest rate on, 143, 146, 148
open-end clauses in, 148
payments on, 143-144, 146
prepayment clauses in, 148
and savings and loan associations, 119-120
Mutual funds, 36, 139
bookkeeping involved, 185
closed-end, 185, 186
commission on buying, 186-187
dividends paid by, 188
government control and regulation, 183-184
and legal list, 183
minimum amount to invest, 184
net assets value, 185-186, 188
open-end, 182, 185-186
operation of, 179-180
past record of, 166
prospectus of, 182
as satisfactory investment, 180-181
selection of, 181-182, 187-188
types of, 182

N

National Association of Securities Dealers, 187
Net asset value, of mutual fund investments, 185-186, 188
Net worth, 34, 38-39
New York Stock Exchange, 161, 165
Nonrecurring income, 41

O

Open-end clause in mortgage, 148

P

Payments
credit, terms of, 69-75
on mortgage, 143-144, 146
Pension plans, 24, 35, 39
Personal liability insurance, 108-109
Personal property
insurance for, 110
record of, 25, 36
value of, 36-37

Portfolio, security
  diversified, 171, 178-179, 184
  of mutual funds, 182
  professional managers of, 168
  "prudent man," 183
Preferred stock, 157-158, 182
Premarital agreement, 30
Premiums, insurance
  benefits of, 99-100
  costs of, 102-103
  disability waiver, 105
  fixed, 101-102
  in term insurance policies, 100-101
Prepayment clauses, in mortgage, 148
Production costs, and inflation, 134
Profit-sharing plans, 24
Property damage
  automobile insurance covering, 107
  homeowners' insurance, 42, 109-110
Prices
  asking, in sale of home, 152, 153, 155-156
  consideration in shopping, 52
  of home, 150-151
  rise in, 86, 133, 134-136
Proxies, 170
Purchasing power, effect of inflation on, 123, 129, 132-133, 138-139

R

Rackets, avoiding, 60-61
Real estate, 35-36, 139-140
  brokers, 154-155
Recreation, spending for, 44
Rent, 41
Repossession, rights of, 76, 77-78
Retirement
  fixed incomes in, and inflation, 133, 139
  investing for, 173-174
Rights, 158

S

Safe deposit box, 26-27, 31
Safes, home, 27
Salary, 40
Sales, 51-53, 67
Saving, 11, 12, 22
  automatic savings plans, 126-128
  by children, 93-94
  by credit buying, 68
  effective methods, 85-86, 125-126
  on home building, 151-152
  long-term programs, 84-86
  motivation for, 127-128
  regular, 174, 175, 190
  on use of credit, 65
  See also Expenses
Savings, 34, 48
  amount, and amount of insurance, 101-102
  deducted from paycheck, 126
  emergency, 113-117, 127, 169
  fixed-dollar, 168-170
  and inflation, 129-133, 138-140

Savings (cont'd.)
insurance for, 118, 119-120, 130
interest on, 130, 137, 138
interest rates on, 117, 118
in life insurance policies, 100, 102
long-term, 113, 129-140, 169
record of, 24
short-term, 113-128, 129
taxes paid on interest, 137, 138
where kept, 116-121
Savings accounts, 126, 130, 168
building, 118
for children, 94
size of, 113-116
Savings and loan associations, 119, 126
Savings banks, 117, 120-121
Savings institutions, types of, 117-121
Securities and Exchange Commission, 183-184
Service charges, on credit, 70, 71
Severance pay, 115
Shares
contractual, 184
mutual fund, 185-187
See also Stocks
Shopping
convenience of, 55-57
self-discipline in, 57-60
"smart," 51-61
use of items bought, 53-55
Social Security, 25-26, 42
Specialty funds, 182
Speculation, 140, 160-161, 177
Spending
adjustable categories, 44
government, and inflation, 133-134, 136
habits, changing, 14-15, 87
personal preferences, 48
power of citizens, 134
Stock advisory services, 163
Stock brokerage firms, 166, 167
Stockbrokers, 166
Stock funds, 182
Stockmarket, 163-164
Stocks, 24, 93-94, 168, 176-178
common, 139, 140, 157-158, 182, 183
diversification in holdings, 171, 178-179, 184
do-it-yourself investing in, 158-165
as long-term investment, 169
market price, 36
preferred, 157-158, 182
purchasing, 158-161, 170-171, 179-188
reasons for buying, 188-190
rise and fall of, 159, 160, 163-164
selling, 39-40
Straight life insurance policies, 100, 101-102, 103

T

Taxes, 38, 123
benefits to government, 189
capital gains, 35-36, 38
deducted from paychecks, 125-126
on home, 41, 42, 146

Taxes (cont'd.)
income, 42, 88-89, 185
on income from mutual funds, 185
and inflation, 133, 134
on interest earned by savings, 137, 138
reduction, 67-68
types of, 42
Tenant's policy, 42
Term insurance, 100-101, 103, 104
decreasing, for mortgage protection, 110
Thrift shops, 54
Tight money, 75
Time, value of, 56-57, 145
Transportation expenses, 43-44, 89, 145, 146
Travel, personal property insurance for, 110
Twenty-payment life insurance policies, 100, 103

U

Unemployment insurance, 42, 114, 116
Uninsured motorist coverage, 108
Unions, labor, 114, 134
U.S. savings bonds, 35, 121-124, 138
Utility bills, 37-38

V

Vital information, keeping list of, 23, 24-26, 31

W

Wages, garnishment, 74-75, 78
Warrants, 158
Wars, and inflation, 134, 138
Widowhood
fixed income in, and inflation, 132-133, 139
insurance payments as support in, 98
money management in, 18
Will, 24
changing, 29
cost of making, 29-30
death without leaving, 27-28
drawing up, 30-31
where kept, 26, 31
Women
and convenience of home, 149
in financial institutions, 21
influence on family spending, 19-21
in labor force, 87-88
life insurance for, 97-98
outside jobs for, 4, 87-91
part-time work for, 90-91
role in money management, 17-19, 21-22, 82, 84
working years of, 19